Valorie Quesenberry

NEVERTHELESS, SHE HAD HOPE for the FUTURE

Inspiring Devotions & Prayers for Women

BARBOUR
PUBLISHING

Published by Barbour Publishing, Inc., 1810 Barbour Drive, Uhrichsville, Ohio 44683, www.barbourbooks.com

Our mission is to inspire the world with the life-changing message of the Bible.

Member of the
Evangelical Christian
Publishers Association

Printed in China.

NEVERTHELESS, HAVE HOPE!

Generally, I like to have evidence for my hope. But the word *nevertheless* gives us a clue into the type of hope we need to have. One dictionary definition says it means "in spite of: notwithstanding." We could say, in the vernacular, "against all odds." This is hope that dares to believe, regardless of what is visible in the present. This is hope that doesn't base its buoyancy on the facts at hand but on the One who knows more facts than we possibly could.

Your future may be unsettled to your eyes. But we are called to live, not by sight but by faith (2 Corinthians 5:7). That literally means that we won't be able to "see" how things are going to be accomplished. But we can live with the certainty that He has it well in hand, in capable Hands, good Hands, never-failing Hands.

As you read these devotions, remember that you are called to audacious, unexplainable, indefatigable, *nevertheless* kind of hope. Look up to the One who makes the impossible possible, and dare to lay out your future before Him. He can make a way.

HOPE FOR STRENGTH

SANDALS OF IRON

*"Your sandals shall be iron and bronze;
as your days, so shall your strength be."*
DEUTERONOMY 33:25 NKJV

God told Moses that he would experience the strength of Jehovah in his ability to keep going day by day. Figuratively (and literally), his shoes wouldn't wear out. He would have the stamina he needed every day for that day's tasks—however great or small.

We know that the same God who led Moses will stand with us today.

What do you need?

What are you facing?

How much strength do you need?

Turn to the One who makes sandals last like iron. He is the day-by-day Provider of strength.

. . . .

*Heavenly Father, I ask today for strength for this day
in my life. You know what I need more than I do. I
am dependent on You. In Jesus' name. Amen.*

PRAISE IN THE ROUTINE

*From the rising of the sun to the going down of it and
from east to west, the name of the Lord is to be praised!*

PSALM 113:3 AMPC

Those who research such things tell us that routines are good
and healthy. Yet, they can be boring; sometimes we dread them.

Keeping hope alive every day in the middle of our never-
ending routines is a challenge. But the psalmist found something
that aided his ability to focus on what is most important—
worship. Even our daily routines can be acts of worship. Worship
is, after all, giving reverence and adoration to God. As we
complete our daily tasks in ways that honor His Word, we may
count it as a kind of worship.

* *

*Father God, today in my routine, I find hope as
I give You praise. Thank You for providing for
me and being the energy in my day. Amen.*

LAUGH AND BE STRONG

"For the joy of the LORD is your strength."
NEHEMIAH 8:10 ESV

A laughing woman is stronger than a sullen one.

To look at everyday life and find something to laugh about takes a strong woman. And the action of laughter generates more strength. Laughing releases good endorphins and helps us process life in a positive way. No, we don't laugh about bad things; we laugh in spite of them.

We don't know if Jesus laughed a lot, but it's not out of character to think He did. Hebrews 12:2 tells us that He endured the cross for future joy. If we endure, by His grace, we will share eternity with Him. And, in the meantime, we can laugh.

. . . .

Father God, thank You for creating me with the ability to laugh. Help me access this powerful tool today for Your glory and my good. Amen.

KEEPING SANE

We can feel fractured in mind and spirit on certain days because of a crammed schedule or personal physical difficulties or relational challenges or a combination of all of it.

We are not promised that life will be, as our grandmothers used to say, "a bed of roses." Being a follower of Christ does not guarantee ease and comfort, but it does give us assurance that He is with us in every moment. The ancient prophet was inspired to write these empowering words—He will keep us in peace if we focus our thoughts on Him. When you are tempted to zero in on still another problem, meet the thought with the confidence that Christ will be there to help you solve it.

• •

*Lord, today I focus my thoughts and my mental responses
on Your sufficiency. Thank You for giving me peace. Amen.*

THE GOOD OLD LIFE

*Older women likewise are to be reverent in
behavior, not slanderers or slaves to much
wine. They are to teach what is good.*

TITUS 2:3 ESV

Have you ever met a woman who was excited about aging? Generally, it's not something we welcome.

But the apostle Paul was divinely inspired to write about older women in his letter to Titus. They are to have good behavior, not spending their time gossiping or drinking (that flies in the face of the retired, living-on-the-golf-course-with-a-glass-of-wine mentality!). And get this, they are to teach good things. One version said, "they should be examples of the good life." Don't you love that? Following God's blueprint gives older women a good life to model for younger women. Talk about strength in aging? That's it!

. . . .

*God, You give me strength in every life season.
Thank You for this good life. Amen.*

NO GUARANTEES
EXCEPT HIS ARMS

The eternal God is thy refuge, and
underneath are the everlasting arms.
DEUTERONOMY 33:27 KJV

Guarantees are a wonderful thing. Sears, Roebuck and Company, started in the late 1890s by Richard W. Sears and Alvah C. Roebuck, was a name synonymous with the "money-back guarantee" for much of the twentieth century. People liked that they could change their mind and be assured they wouldn't lose their investment.

As Christians, we have no guarantees of easy living or a hefty bank accounts or protection from hardship. We are subject to all the ills of our fallen world just like anyone else. But we do have the guarantee of His presence as our constant refuge. There is no situation on earth in which He cannot bring good in the end. And even Sears couldn't promise that.

• •

Heavenly Father, thank You for the promise of Your
arms of strength around me in any situation. Amen.

UNCHANGING, EVER FAITHFUL

"For I the Lord do not change."
MALACHI 3:6 ESV

Jesus Christ is the same yesterday and today and forever.
HEBREWS 13:8 ESV

You will change [the heavens] like a robe, and they will pass away, but you are the same, and your years have no end.
PSALM 102:26–27 ESV

The greatest source of strength for the woman who loves God is the fact that she can trust in His unchangeability. Humans change, nature changes, cultures and societies change, but He does not. He dwells outside of time and change. He is the constant Same, the eternal Always. He will be the same tomorrow as today and the same next week as He was last year. We can put our confidence in that and find hope for all our *nevertheless* moments.

* *

O Lord, I praise You because You are unchanging and ever faithful. Keep me centered today. In Jesus' name. Amen.

SOLAR STRENGTHENING

Light is sweet, and it is pleasant
for the eyes to see the sun.
ECCLESIASTES 11:7 ESV

The sun was created by God to be a source of strength for us. Early pagan peoples often misguidedly worshipped the sun itself instead of the One who made it. But our Creator spoke the sun into existence for our strengthening—it causes the earth to bloom through the process of photosynthesis; it warms the planet so we can exist; its rays on our heads cause the production of serotonin (the happy hormone) in our bodies. The appearance of the sun each new day reminds us that God is in charge of our world. It reminds us of redemption—God can lighten anything we bring to Him in surrender. And that gives us needed strength.

· ·

Lord God, You have made the sun to remind
me of You. Today, I ask for Your strength. Amen.

HIS HOLY NATURE
IS OUR STRENGTH

*Your decrees are very trustworthy; holiness
befits your house, O LORD, forevermore.*
PSALM 93:5 ESV

Holiness is a frightening term to some. It seems to signify a rigid and aloof character, an exacting manner that angrily tosses out anyone who isn't a goody-two-shoes.

Actually, holiness is the most important attribute of our God. If He were not perfectly holy, He would not love us as He does. Because there is no guile or imperfection in Him, He is compassionate and longsuffering, even as He does not lower His standards in compromise. If He were not totally holy, we would wonder if He were being capricious or malicious or disingenuous when bad things happen to us. But we can trust His actions because we can trust His nature.

* *

*Lord God, thank You for being holy in
all You do and are. I trust You. Amen.*

STRENGTH IN FAMILY

So then you are no longer strangers and aliens,
but you are fellow citizens with the saints and
members of the household of God.
EPHESIANS 2:19 ESV

One's biological family can be a network of strength or a system of pain; some produce strong children and others develop children who possess abnormal and unhealthy perspectives.

We are commanded in scripture to be part of the family of God, a local church body, because He knows we need the strength of being in community with those who have the same Father and who live by the same covenant. We are to practice redemption and hope so that our corner of this great family is a network of ongoing strength.

. . . .

God, guide me as I interact in my local church. Help me to be
a voice of support and redemption. In Jesus' name. Amen.

HOPE FOR FAMILY

PRAYING FOR A PRODIGAL

A foolish son is a sorrow to his mother.
PROVERBS 10:1 ESV

Children bring joy to their mothers when they listen and obey and honor them. But when they flaunt their rebellion and turn their backs on the guiding principles of their home, they bring grief to their moms. Perhaps today you are praying for a wayward child.

Prodigals come in every kind of package—from bad homes, from good homes, from rich and poor homes, from the country and from the city, from quiet settings and from boisterous backgrounds, from every church denomination, every personality, and every generation. What they have in common is a disdain for authority.

Don't give up. Keep praying. Keep throwing your hope on the God who redeems prodigals.

. . . .

Father, right now I pray that You will overcome my child's resistance to truth and bring him home. In Jesus' name. Amen.

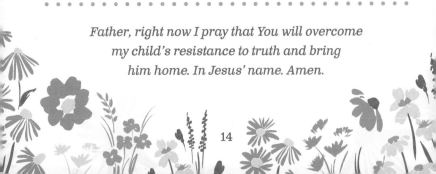

GETTING THE BEST
AS AN IN-LAW

Then Naomi her mother-in-law said to Ruth, My daughter,
shall I not seek rest or a home for you, that you may prosper?
RUTH 3:1 AMPC

Perhaps no other human family relationship is susceptible to teasing like that of mother-in-law. And there are challenges to loving a mom who didn't raise you or to loving a child you didn't raise. But once again, the Bible gives us a clue into how to tap into a good in-law relationship:

Seek their best.

Whichever side you are on—mother or adult child—seek ways to make the other prosper, to give them joy and comfort, as Naomi did for Ruth. It might not win them in one day, but over time, it just might.

. . . .

Lord, You designed families, and You know
how to help me relate to my in-laws. I ask
for Your wisdom and joy in doing it. Amen.

GOD OF DELIVERANCE

*Oh, let the wickedness of the wicked come
to an end, but establish the [uncompromisingly]
righteous [those upright and in harmony with You].*
PSALM 7:9 AMPC

Pornography is available to everyone these days because of technology. And the statistics are alarming. The world is horribly stained with illicit sexual pleasure.

Someone you know is ensnared by this. Perhaps today your heart is heavy as you remember their promises to keep clean, which are soon broken, or their inability to think of relationships in natural ways.

You can pray the words of the psalmist. Let this wickedness come to an end. And pray that God will bring misery on the sinning one until he or she repents. And while you pray, hope, because the God of deliverance hears you.

. . . .

*Lord God, my loved one is drowning in wickedness.
Bring misery and conviction and then deliverance.
Let a heart-change happen. In Jesus' name. Amen.*

A HAVEN WHILE IN TRANSITION

Be to me a rock of refuge,
to which I may continually come.
PSALM 71:3 ESV

Moving to another location involves not only hard work but also emotional upheaval. Some families experience this regularly; others may only experience it once or twice in their family's life. Some never do.

But if you are in the process of moving or if you know someone who is, it is good to be reminded that uprooting and relocating isn't something simply done. It is complex. It affects almost every aspect of personal and family life.

Women have a strong need for security, for domestic constancy. Moving is a challenge to that need. The Word of God tells us that He is our refuge where we may come continually. That's good news, wherever we are currently living.

. . . .

Lord, thank You for being a continuous refuge. Give me
strength and hope in my uprooted moments. Amen.

CONFLICT ISN'T THE END

Accept life, and be most patient and tolerant with one another,
always ready to forgive if you have a difference with anyone.
COLOSSIANS 3:13 PHILLIPS

It's just not realistic to think that we will live everyday life without some conflict somewhere. But, as women of God, we have hope even in moments of conflict.

The Gospel is life-changing and life-empowering. God, through the power of Jesus' shed blood, changes us from the inside out and then gives us the Holy Spirit to help us live a new kind of life. Because of this empowerment, we can follow what the apostle Paul wrote—patience, tolerance, and forgiveness. That turns conflict into an opportunity to grow in personal discipline. What a win!

. . . .

Lord Jesus, You modeled for us how to live
patiently and mercifully with even those who
hated You. Help me to do the same. Amen.

MORE THAN SMILES AND HUGS

But the mercy of the LORD is from everlasting
to everlasting on those who fear Him, and
His righteousness to children's children.
PSALM 103:17 NKJV

Grandmas love to spend time with their grandchildren. They love the sweet, clear eyes and the chubby little arms that hug their necks. They love the stubby little legs that run to greet them when they visit and the toothy little grins that light up small faces.

But the woman who has hope for the future wants to see her grandchildren follow the God of heaven with a devoted heart and experience His mercy and righteousness. And she prays for that to happen with every visit, with every interaction with those beloved children. She looks ahead and hopes through prayer.

* *

Heavenly Father, thank You for creating the idea of
grandmothering. Help me today to hope for the future
through my intercession for my grandchildren. Amen.

FINDING SAFETY

He will cover you with his pinions, and under his wings you
will find refuge; his faithfulness is a shield and buckler.

PSALM 91:4 ESV

Women care about safety. Wives are usually the ones who prod
their husbands to visit doctors for health checkups. Mothers
are usually the ones who call out "be careful" to their teenage
children taking out the family car.

We women can be overcome with fears about our own safety
and that of those we love. While scripture speaks to both men
and women on the subject of trusting God, women may find
the verses specifically applicable.

. . . .

Father in heaven, I'm glad You are protection I
can trust and that Your eyes don't miss anything
that is happening to my family. Amen.

VIBRANT SPIRITUAL FAMILY LIFE

So shall they be life unto thy soul, and grace to thy neck.
PROVERBS 3:22 KJV

Women are hardwired by God to care deeply about family matters, and that includes the spiritual health of those we love. If you think about your own family heritage, you will probably remember a grandmother or aunt or mother who prayed for you and encouraged you with little talks about following God and living right.

As we raise our own families, we become the encouragers and prayers. Whatever season your family is in, whatever your marital status, no doubt there is someone you love for whom you are praying.

The writer of Proverbs tells us to prioritize wisdom and it will adorn our lives. This is what we want to pass on to our loved ones.

Father God, I ask You to open the eyes of my family members to godly wisdom. In Jesus' name. Amen.

THE TREMBLING HOUSE

Man is going to his eternal home.
ECCLESIASTES 12:5 ESV

One of the most difficult experiences for us women is to watch our parents grow old. We are becoming the caregivers, the protectors. It's an odd reversal of roles.

When we see them begin to fade away, little by little, we can have hope for their future as we look to the solidity of eternal truth. Ecclesiastes 12 speaks of the arms trembling and the legs bowing and the teeth falling out, the eyes darkening and the hearing diminishing. But verse seven reminds us that the spirit will return to the God who gave it. Those who have put their trust in Christ need not fear for themselves or for their aging parents. His house is forever.

. . . .

Father, I bring my parents to You today and trust them to Your eternal care. In Jesus' name. Amen.

22

THE *D* WORD

*"For the man who does not love his wife
but divorces her, says the LORD, the God of
Israel, covers his garment with violence,
says the LORD of hosts. So guard yourselves
in your spirit, and do not be faithless."*

MALACHI 2:16 ESV

Little girls, teen girls, young women dream about their wedding day. And no woman wants to be abandoned, unloved, or treated badly. No woman sets out in life hoping to experience the horror of divorce.

God hates divorce, hates what it does to His creation. But He always offers hope to those scarred by it, forgiveness for bad decisions, healing for wounds caused by another. If you have experienced divorce, look to Him instead of to another magazine article. Find hope in His truth and love.

. . . .

*Dear Lord, give me hope today in place
of despair. In Jesus' name. Amen.*

HOPE FOR A LIFE MISSION
HOPE IN HARDSHIP—
ANN HASSELTINE JUDSON

And you will feel secure, because there is hope; you
will look around and take your rest in security.

JOB 11:18 ESV

Born in 1789 in Massachusetts to a respected and wealthy family, Ann lived a carefree and spoiled life until the age of 16 when she was converted to faith in Christ in a revival wave sweeping up and down the New England Coast. She married Adoniram Judson in 1812 and they set off as missionaries, ending up in what was then called Burma, modern-day Myanmar. There, bringing the Gospel to unreached peoples, she suffered privation, loneliness, unbearable heat, government persecution, the imprisonment of her husband, the death of two babies, sickness, and finally her own death, followed by the death of her only living child, Maria.

She and Adoniram and another couple who traveled with them were the first American foreign missionaries. Hope in hardship is the knowledge that no trial here compares to the glory There.

* *

God of mission, send me to tell Your
Gospel to someone today. Amen.

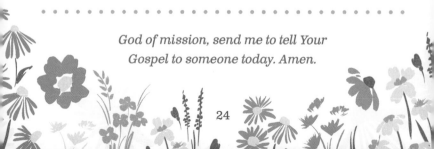

HOPE IN CHALLENGES—
GLADYS AYLWARD

Blessed (happy, fortunate, to be envied) are the
undefiled (the upright, truly sincere, and blameless)
in the way [of the revealed will of God], who walk
(order their conduct and conversation) in the law
of the Lord (the whole of God's revealed will).

PSALM 119:1 AMPC

She was a parlor maid in London who failed her examinations at the China Inland Mission Center. Still convinced that God wanted her to take the Gospel to China, she set off on her own and made the arduous way by rail, boat, bus, and mule, finally arriving in China in 1930 to work as an assistant to Mrs. Jeannie Lawson.

The two women ran a roadside inn—offering food, water, sustenance for the mules, and stories about Jesus. After Mrs. Lawson's death, Gladys continued to share the Gospel. She began adopting orphans and saved them in a daring rescue from the advance of enemy armies during World War II.

Hope in challenges holds fast to the belief that God is always watching over those who do His will.

Lord God, if You can use a parlor maid, You can
use me. Give me hope in my challenges. Amen.

HOPE IN ADVERSITY—
FANNY J. CROSBY

*In the day of prosperity be joyful, but in the day
of adversity consider that God has made the one
side by side with the other, so that man may not
find out anything that shall be after him.*

ECCLESIASTES 7:14 AMPC

It was a doctor's accident that made Fanny Crosby blind at the age of six weeks. But she never indulged in resentment against him. Rather, she invested her life in what she could do, memorizing great portions of the Bible, playing guitar, piano, organ, and harp and, of course, writing poetry. She is credited with composing between 8,000 and 9,000 verses, many of which were set to music as hymns under her own name and her various pseudonyms.

She married one of her students at the New York Institute of the Blind, and together they had one child who died in infancy. She died at the age of 94 in 1915, having had a personal goal to win one million souls to Christ through her hymns.

Hope in adversity means not allowing life's assaults to dim the effect of God's gifts in you.

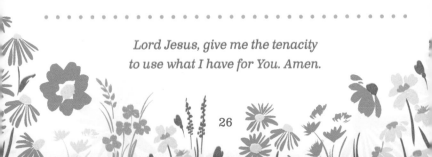

*Lord Jesus, give me the tenacity
to use what I have for You. Amen.*

HOPE IN CALLING—
RUTH BELL GRAHAM

*"Set your heart on the kingdom and his goodness, and
all these things will come to you as a matter of course."*
MATTHEW 6:33 PHILLIPS

The name Billy Graham is well-known to many people. His wife,
Ruth, was an integral part of his ministry as well as having
influence of her own.

She was born in China to missionary parents and early
on recognized her own calling to help share the Gospel with
others. After marrying Billy in 1943, she went on to be not only
his trusted confidante and sweetheart, but also a helper to him
in his ministry while raising their five children, authoring
many books, and loving whomever God put in her way.

Hope in one's calling means knowing what is most important
and letting that direct everything else.

* *

*Lord, give me a heart that is centered
on what is most important—You. Amen.*

HOPE IN DOMESTICITY— SUSANNA WESLEY

Therefore I desire that the younger widows marry, bear children, manage the house.
1 TIMOTHY 5:14 NKJV

Susanna Wesley is best known as the mother of John and Charles Wesley, founder of Methodism, and hymn writer, respectively. But this remarkable woman gave birth to nineteen children following her marriage to Samuel Wesley at age 19 in 1688. It was she who was responsible for their incredible spiritual training in addition to keeping the home running during her husband's imprisonment in debtors' prison, through the tragedies of two house fires and years of poverty and struggle.

She is remembered for her insightful methods of child-rearing and her faithfulness to catechize them in theology and piety. Much of the success of her famous sons is credited to her.

Hope in domesticity means understanding that the calling to raise children is God's work.

* * *

Father, impress on me the value of a God-centered home and help me to create one. In Jesus' name. Amen.

HOPE IN PROMISE—
NETTIE PEABODY

*She considered [God] Who had given her the promise
to be reliable and trustworthy and true to His word.*
HEBREWS 11:11 AMPC

She was first a student and then a professor at a small Bible college in the city of Cincinnati.

In the early 1950s, when a financial crisis loomed over the campus and confiscation of property seemed imminent, Nettie prayed into the night for her beloved school. She felt that God gave her the words of Joshua 1:3 as her own, that every place "the sole of her foot" would walk would be saved from foreclosure. Years later, the Bible college still exists, and none of the property over which she prayed, and on which she marched in triumph, has been lost.

Hope in promise means looking to God to interpret His Word in His time.

* *

*Lord God, You are faithful and good.
I look to You for security. Amen.*

HOPE IN DEATH—BETTY STAM

So now also Christ shall be magnified in
my body, whether it be by life, or by death.
PHILIPPIANS 1:20 KJV

A woman's greatest fear, even greater than for her own life, is for the safety of her child. Betty Scott Stam faced both of these fears at the end of her short missionary life.

Born to missionary parents in Michigan and raised in China, Betty returned to Asia herself after college. She married fellow student and missionary John Stam and worked alongside him in a small Chinese village where communist soldiers claimed control in December 1934. Betty and John were paraded through the streets in their undergarments, held overnight in a secluded location, and then executed. Baby Helen Priscilla, hidden in heavy winter blankets by Betty and protected by the heavenly Father, survived, unharmed.

Hope in death means knowing that what comes after death is real life.

. . . .

Lord Jesus, give me Your presence in the hour
of my death and be glorified in me. Amen.

HOPE IN THE UNEXPECTED—
KATHARINE VON BORA LUTHER

*But thanks be to God, who in Christ always leads us
in triumphal procession, and through us spreads the
fragrance of the knowledge of him everywhere.*
2 CORINTHIANS 2:14 ESV

Her life was to run the expected course once she entered the
Benedictine cloister in 1504 to further her education under
the eye of her aunt. Eventually, she became a nun. But
Katharine grew discontented with monastic life and more
interested in the new reform movement gaining attention.
She took drastic action when she escaped from the convent
along with eleven other nuns with the help of none other
than Martin Luther himself.

She married Luther in 1525, and together they forged a
joyful life, parenting six biological children plus adopted ones.

Hope in the unexpected means accepting God's surprises
with anticipation of His provision.

* *

*God, I trust You to show me when to accept
the unexpected from Your hand. Amen.*

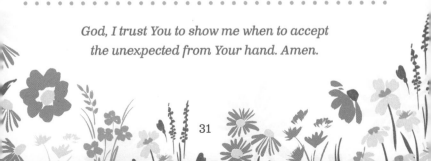

HOPE IN DARING MOMENTS— AMY CARMICHAEL

Rescuing young girls from prostitution in a Hindu temple under the noses of the authorities and with the threat of legal ramifications is justifiably considered daring. And it is a calling for which her childhood inclination to thrills and practical jokes uniquely qualified her, along with her brown eyes (which she once desperately prayed would change to blue) and dark hair enabling her to mingle unsuspected with the people.

Amy Carmichael was born in 1867 in Ireland and did mission work both in the London slums and in Japan before settling in India, serving there over fifty-five years and coming to be known as "Amma" (mother) to hundreds of children.

Hope in daring moments means taking righteous action to help others in Christ's name.

* *

Father God, use me to accomplish
daring things in Your will. Amen.

HOPE IN SUFFERING— CORRIE TEN BOOM

Cornelia Arnolda Johanna ten Boom was born in 1892. Her family was deeply involved in living out the Gospel in acts of goodness in society, and Corrie herself had a ministry for mentally challenged children. When Nazi occupation came to Holland, Corrie and her family ran a safehouse for Jews.

Betrayed, arrested, sent to prison (where her father died), transported to a concentration camp (where her sister Betsie died), Corrie suffered the worst kinds of abuse humans can inflict on others. Released due to a clerical "error" at the age of 53, Corrie traveled the world sharing God's message of forgiveness and healing and hope.

Hope in suffering means finding the source of strength in One who suffered more.

. . . .

Lord, when I suffer, may I remember to place my fate in Your nail-scarred hands. Amen.

HOPE IN LOSS—ELISABETH ELLIOT

*And after you have borne these sufferings a very little
while, God himself (from whom we receive all grace
and who has called you to share his eternal splendour
through Christ) will make you whole and secure and
strong. All power is his for ever and ever, amen!*
1 PETER 5:10–11 PHILLIPS

Maybe no missionary account has gripped the mind and emotion
more than the story of five missionary men martyred for the
Gospel in the jungles of Ecuador. Elisabeth's first husband,
Jim Elliot, was one of them. Her second husband, theologian
Addison Leach, died of cancer.

Her significant losses gave her an unusual platform for
her gifts in writing and speaking. She always maintained that
suffering was not "for nothing."

Hope in loss means that God is the only treasure that can
never be taken, and He will eternally remain.

· ·

*Heavenly Father, when I must relinquish what
is dear, remind me to hold fast to You. Amen.*

HOPE FOR WISDOM

DON'T LIVE WITHOUT IT

Wisdom is the principal thing; therefore get wisdom.
And in all your getting, get understanding.

PROVERBS 4:7 NKJV

Wisdom is important for everyday living. According to the wise writer of Proverbs, inspired by the Holy Spirit, wisdom is the chief attribute we should desire. For, when we are truly wise, we will choose to follow Christ, the Source of wisdom, and we will guide our lives by His Word.

Wisdom in everyday life will help us in all the little decisions too—what to wear, who to encourage, when to keep silent instead of speaking, when to show love to someone who doesn't deserve it, and in so many other situations.

. . . .

Lord God, You are the supreme fount of wisdom and I
ask You to bless me with a greater measure of it. Amen.

INTUITION GUIDED BY THE SPIRIT

And blessed is your advice and blessed are you, because
you have kept me this day from coming to bloodshed
and from avenging myself with my own hand.

1 SAMUEL 25:33 NKJV

Abigail was a woman of beauty and discretion. The Bible tells us that's a winning combination. Not all of us have beauty, but we can all own discretion with the help of God's Word and the direction of the Holy Spirit. Abigail faced a possibly disastrous situation and was used by God in a wise way to avert the wrath of David on her husband and all the male servants who worked for him.

You may not ever help avoid an actual battle, but you can be used by God to diffuse tempers and allay fears and bring solutions. You can access wisdom for daily living!

* *

Thank You, God, for the gift of Your Word
and the guidance of the Holy Spirit. Amen.

CALMNESS FROM THE LORD

But his wife said to him, "If the LORD had desired to kill us, He would not have accepted a burnt offering and a grain offering from our hands, nor would He have shown us all these things, nor would He have told us such things as these at this time."

JUDGES 13:23 NKJV

The wife of Manoah saw an angel who told her that her infertility was over and that she would give birth to a son. Like a wise wife, she told her husband and then the angel visited them a second time. When he miraculously ascended into heaven, Manoah was afraid, convinced they would die. But his wife gentled his fears with her wise words.

Today, maybe you can give someone hope and offer someone calmness with your wise words.

* *

God, make me Your mouthpiece today to say wise and calming words. In Christ's name. Amen.

THINK NOTHING OF IT

Good sense makes one slow to anger,
and it is his glory to overlook an offense.
PROVERBS 19:11 ESV

It has been said that to say "Oh, that's okay" when another voices an apology is actually avoiding the act of forgiveness by passing it off without acknowledging the transgression and the need to extend mercy.

But the other side of that coin is the Spirit-empowered ability to "overlook" an offense when the party doesn't offer an apology. This is equally hard to do.

Yet, wisdom, godly wisdom, helps us to recognize that some things just aren't worth the spiritual cost to ourselves and our future. We can overlook a lot more things than we think we can. We don't have to be petty and vengeful. We can, instead, be filled with the Spirit and show mercy.

• •

Lord God, empower me today through Your
Spirit to overlook many offenses. Amen.

FIRST THING IN THE MORNING

She opens her mouth with wisdom.
PROVERBS 31:26 ESV

What are the first words out of your mouth in the morning? Do they set the tone for the day?

It's an interesting thought, isn't it?

The tried-and-true "Good morning" might be a nice start to your daily vocal activity, voiced to a family member, or a pet if you live alone, or better yet to God Himself!

Many of the attributes of the woman described in Proverbs 31 seem unattainable (though actually this chapter wasn't meant to be a way to bludgeon women every Mother's Day, but rather a sort of praise sheet for the many honorable ways in which good women serve). Yet, one that all of us can actually do is to purposefully field and focus our words in kind ways.

. . . .

Heavenly Father, give me the purpose of heart
to open my mouth with wisdom. Amen.

BE CAREFUL WHAT YOU REQUEST

She said to him, "Say that these two sons of mine are to sit,
one at your right hand and one at your left, in your kingdom."
Jesus answered, "You do not know what you are asking."
MATTHEW 20:21–22 ESV

Most mothers want the best for their own children and many
ask the Lord to bless their children in special ways. But perhaps
we need to use godly wisdom in our requests.

A woman named Salome who had two strong and gifted
sons asked Jesus for favor on them. She wanted them to be
blessed, to be used by the Master. But Jesus knew that she
didn't understand the details of what she was asking. She was
asking unwisely. We sometimes do the same.

. . . .

Lord God, forgive me for requesting unwise blessings
for my children. Please guide my prayers. Amen.

HUSBAND FOR HIRE

And Jacob came out of the field in the evening, and
Leah went out to meet him and said, You must sleep
with me [tonight], for I have certainly paid your hire with
my son's mandrakes. So he slept with her that night.
GENESIS 30:16 AMPC

It sounds like a modern-day soap opera plot. Two sisters, one plain and one beautiful, married to the same man. The plain one has many children; the beautiful one is infertile. And then, in an exchange with her sister for some herbs that were alleged to have fertility qualities, plain Leah manipulates her husband into spending the night in her tent.

How many times have you been tempted to use manipulation instead of godly wisdom? It won't cause your difficult person to love you. Don't try to hire out your solution; ask God to help you.

. . . .

Lord, keep me from foolishly trying to manipulate
people instead of asking You for help. Amen.

SPINNING WITH WISDOM

All the women who had ability and were wisehearted
spun with their hands and brought what they had spun
of blue and purple and scarlet [stuff] and fine linen;
and all the women who had ability and whose hearts
stirred them up in wisdom spun the goats' hair.
EXODUS 35:25–26 AMPC

The people of Israel had been delivered from their captivity in Egypt by the mighty hand of God. They were learning how to worship the one true God. Moses told them God's words concerning the construction of the Tabernacle of worship. Skillful craftsmen and artisans donated their time to help bring it to completion. Among these were wise women who had ability; they spun the goats' hair and they spun it into fine linen.

What can you do for God today? Do you have an ability? Be wise and use it!

. . . .

God of all gifts, I want to be wise and
use my talents in Your service. Amen.

A TEST OF WISDOM

*When the queen of Sheba heard of the fame of Solomon,
she came to Jerusalem to test him with hard questions,
accompanied by very many attendants and camels bearing
spices, much gold, and precious stones. And when she came
to Solomon, she talked with him of all that was on her mind.*

2 CHRONICLES 9:1 AMPC

Our questions help us test our knowledge and gain a clearer
grasp of the content.

The Queen of Sheba wanted to see for herself if the stories
she had heard of Solomon's wisdom and riches were true. So
she came for a visit and asked questions. And because of it, she
gained more wisdom and a new friend and ally.

• •

*O God, You are greater by far than Solomon. You are the One
who gave him wisdom. I will bring my questions to You. Amen.*

NOTHING APART FROM GOD

All this have I tried and proved by wisdom. I said, I will
be wise [independently of God]—but it was far from me.
ECCLESIASTES 7:23 AMPC

Culture often touts the wisdom of celebrities and CEOs and other influencers who are popular in the moment. Their words on how to build a business, make money, create a following, craft a brand, structure a portfolio and more are printed, published, and quoted. Their interviews are sought-after, and their names are desired for advertising. But if they seek to be wise independently of God, they will ultimately fail in the business of eternity.

Building a life and making decisions based on the solid wisdom of God is the key to lasting success. The wisdom writer of scripture was inspired to remind us that there is no true wisdom apart from Him.

. . . .

Lord God, today I seek Your eternal wisdom. Amen.

HOPE FOR CALAMITIES
CALM IN THE STORM

He hushes the storm to a calm and to a gentle
whisper, so that the waves of the sea are still.
PSALM 107:29 AMPC

Perhaps you have been on the water when a storm blew in. Today, we usually have advance warning of bad weather. In Bible times, they didn't. They relied more on their senses and their instincts honed from years of experience.

One of the well-known miracles of Jesus is the calming of the storm that arose on the Sea of Galilee. And how often we find ourselves in a sudden storm—a health crisis, a family emergency, a relationship drama, a ministry challenge, an emotional disruption. In these times, we can turn to the One who "hushes the storm." It may still howl around us, but in our spirits, He whispers gently and holds us securely.

. . . .

Lord Jesus, You stilled the storm for
the disciples; quiet mine today. Amen.

COMFORT FROM ABOVE

This is my comfort in my affliction,
that your promise gives me life.
PSALM 119:50 ESV

How do you spell comfort?

Is it a favorite blanket, a comfy chair by the fire, a hot drink, a back porch, a supportive pillow, a favorite pair of slippers? It is interesting that often our physical comforts are tied to a sensory experience—something we feel, taste, or smell. Tactile comfort is a real thing. But there are times when no tactile comfort is sufficient. There are certain tragedies that seem to flout our efforts to find comfort and even make us feel guilty for looking for it.

The psalmist knew that genuine comfort only comes from God in these kinds of times. He knew that the promises of the Bible give hope for life.

• •

O God, only You bring real comfort in extreme
circumstances. I look to You. Amen.

SALTED OR SWEETENED

You are a hiding place for me; you preserve me from
trouble; you surround me with shouts of deliverance.
PSALM 32:7 ESV

Our grandmothers often canned preserves—of fruits and vegetables. What was needed was a preserving agent to keep the fresh substance from decaying. Sometimes salt was used; other times, sugar was employed. And the wonderful result gave us delighted tummies for months to come.

God is into preserving His saints in times of trouble. Sometimes He uses salt—the trial irritates us but makes us better because of the action of the briny pain involved. Sometimes He works through pleasant means—protection from the worst, a sweet and miraculous answer. But either way, He is using the best means at that moment to preserve us and keep us fresh for eternity.

. . . .

Heavenly Father, thank You for preserving me
in the way You know is best right now. Amen.

TRUST THE ANCHOR

This hope we hold as the utterly reliable anchor for
our souls, fixed in the very certainty of God himself in
Heaven, where Jesus has already entered on our behalf.
HEBREWS 6:19–20 PHILLIPS

In our day of air travel, we aren't as familiar with the imagery of anchors. But in the day when these words were penned, the average person knew the importance of an anchor. Ships were the major means of international transport, and many people to whom the New Testament epistles were written lived along sea routes. Anchors keep large ships from drifting in the water and secure them during stormy blasts.

Our hope in Christ is the anchor of our souls. When life's calamities pile on us, our trust in Him keeps us upright and secure.

. . . .

Lord Jesus, I cast myself into Your keeping
and trust You as a ship does its anchor. Amen.

FUEL FOR LIFE

Three times I begged the Lord for it to leave me, but
his reply has been, "My grace is enough for you: for where
there is weakness, my power is shown the more completely."

2 CORINTHIANS 12:8–9 PHILLIPS

It has been said that grace is the Christian's fuel for life. There are two types of grace—one is the merciful favor of salvation through the blood of Christ, and the other is the divine enablement to meet the challenges of life. It is the latter kind that Paul references in the scripture above.

Grace, the gift of strength from God, is available to us anywhere, anytime, in any measure. We can never exhaust the supply. We can never ask too often. In fact, usually we fail to ask for enough of it.

Today, in your moment of calamity, cry out to God for grace. It's there.

. . . .

Father, I depend on heaven's fuel
today. In Jesus' name. Amen.

A MATTER OF POISE

*Strength and dignity are her clothing
and her position is strong and secure.*
PROVERBS 31:25 AMPC

In previous centuries, young girls were often sent to "finishing schools" where they were "finished" or polished, receiving careful instruction in refinement and proper social graces. Poise would have been at the top of the list. It was demonstrated by actions like always speaking in even tones, even in times of excitement or strain, and in never turning to stare or acting baffled by another's social faux pas.

Today, we still value another woman's ability to keep her cool and act with strength and dignity in difficult situations. The Bible also praises this ability and tells us at the end of the chapter that dependence on the Lord makes these virtues possible.

. . . .

*God, I want to be a woman of poise even in
calamity. Give me that kind of strength. Amen.*

WAITING OUT THE STORM

Be merciful to me, O God, be merciful to me, for in
you my soul takes refuge; in the shadow of your wings
I will take refuge, till the storms of destruction pass by.

PSALM 57:1 ESV

If you picture in your mind a place of refuge, what would it be?

In earlier days, almost every farm in the blustery region of the country had a storm cellar, a subterranean shelter with an entrance often covered by a door and leading downward by steps into the earth. There, the family would retreat when a cyclone was spotted on the horizon, taking refuge until the storms passed.

There may be a twister headed your way today. Head for your refuge in Christ and wait out the storm in His strength.

• •

Lord of Refuge, I run to You today. Hide
me in the shadow of Your wings. Amen.

51

MADE FOR A PURPOSE

And we know that for those who love God
all things work together for good, for those
who are called according to his purpose.
ROMANS 8:28 ESV

Just as human products are meant to fulfill some purpose, so are human beings designed by their Creator. Before any of us came to be, our God had in His mind a distinct purpose for each one. First of all, we are purposed to be in relationship with Him, and He accomplished this through the sacrificial death of His Son. Second, we are purposed to bring Him glory in the unique ways He gives us. These purposes hold true even in the midst of calamity and tragedy.

. . . .

Holy Father, thank You for making me for a
specific purpose. Help me hold fast to it. Amen.

LEANING ON THE RIGHT SUPPORT

The LORD is my strength and my
song; he has become my salvation.
PSALM 118:14 ESV

One of the common maladies in later years is back pain. After supporting our spines and helping us walk and lift and perform all manner of other actions, the back often lets us know that it is tired and sometimes injured. The skeletal structure and muscular system that God designed are amazing, but wear and tear and sometimes an unwise move or two can cause them to malfunction. The support we thought we had is gone.

Often, in times of duress, we find that our earthly networks of support are incapable of holding our weight. They malfunction and let us down. But the strength we gain from our trust in God is unfailing. It will hold us forever.

. . . .

Lord God, thank You for the support I find
in Your strength. I lean on You today. Amen.

AVOIDING WORRY

[Wisdom's] ways are highways of
pleasantness, and all her paths are peace.
PROVERBS 3:17 AMPC

"Don't worry; be happy" used to be a popular catchphrase. But in the middle of our distresses, peace seems far away. When we receive shocking news or experience an unexpected crisis, our immediate tendency is toward anxiety and fear. And this is a natural human reaction. The only way to change that visceral response is with the solid help of the Lord. When we depend on His wisdom, we can move toward peace.

The Bible tells us that His peace comes from looking at life through His perspective and by trusting His providential care and His sovereign will at work in our lives.

* *

Heavenly Father, the only way I can avoid
worry is to trust Your wisdom about my
future. By Your grace, I do that today. Amen.

A SPIRITUAL WORKOUT

Behold, we consider those blessed who remained
steadfast. You have heard of the steadfastness of
Job, and you have seen the purpose of the Lord,
how the Lord is compassionate and merciful.
JAMES 5:11 ESV

Those who run marathons need endurance. They cannot sprint the distance. They cannot use up their stores of strength in the first mile. They have to pace themselves and remain steadfast.

Building the personal stamina to endure the grueling workout of a marathon takes time and discipline. So does building spiritual stamina. It is the result of many hours and days of submitting to the discipline of the Word and enduring the workout of the Spirit as He corrects us and guides us. But the end result is the ability to run a steadfast race, even in hard times.

. . . .

God, keep me in the spiritual workout I need to
improve my stamina in trials. In Jesus' name. Amen.

HOPE FOR FRIENDSHIPS

SOLID GOLD

A friend loves at all times.
PROVERBS 17:17 AMPC

God is the Creator of friendship. He designed the components and types of earthly relationship, from marriage and the family to comrades and confidantes. And friendship done His way involves kindness and loyalty, loving at all times, no matter what.

A true friend doesn't value her reputation more than her friendship with you or your opinion of her rather than truth. A true friend is unfailingly kind but surprisingly honest.

If you want to invest in friendships that last and become solid gold, practice what you want her to do. Never turn your back on her, even if she disappoints you, and always frame your friendship with kindness. It will bring great rewards.

. . . .

Lord, thank You for creating friendship. Guide
me in being a never-failing friend. Amen.

BEING A BRAVE FRIEND

Faithful are the wounds of a friend;
profuse are the kisses of an enemy.
PROVERBS 27:6 ESV

Being a real friend requires bravery. It isn't enough to like to giggle at the same silly things and to enjoy the same type of latte and to give compliments when one of you is feeling down. Friendship requires honesty and, at times, difficult honesty.

Giving your friend a true evaluation of her need or giving her honest feedback on a delicate matter isn't for the faint of heart. You will need to square your shoulders, pray for the right words, and proceed with gentleness. You will need to be brave.

This scripture can help remind you that it is better to help your friend through a healing wound than it is to cover over problems with flattery. May you ever be a brave friend.

. . . .

Lord God, You are faithful and
honest with me. I love You. Amen.

57

GENERATIONAL LOYALTY

*Then Jonathan said to David, "Go in peace, because
we have sworn both of us in the name of the Lord,
saying, 'The Lord shall be between me and you, and
between my offspring and your offspring, forever.' "*
1 SAMUEL 20:42 ESV

The friendship of David and Jonathan is an enduring example
of loyalty and tenacity. King Saul was obsessed with killing
David, ending what he considered to be a threat to his throne
and his legacy through the prince Jonathan. Yet, despite the fact
that Saul and his sons would not reign, Jonathan was David's
best friend and even an ally against his father's schemes.

Probably none of your friendships have this kind of
backdrop, yet there are many strains that come against
friendship. Resolve that you will be the kind of friend who
pledges faithfulness even to your children's generation.

* *

*Lord, give me understanding and integrity
so I may be a true friend. Amen.*

GET HER TO JESUS

And they came, bringing to him a paralytic carried
by four men. And when they could not get near him
because of the crowd, they removed the roof above
him, and when they had made an opening, they
let down the bed on which the paralytic lay.
MARK 2:3–4 ESV

These guys didn't let the inconvenience, the hardship, or the weird looks from other people stop them from not only carrying his bed but also from taking apart the roof to lower his bed into the house.

As a friend, there may be ways you can serve that will not be easy or convenient. You may feel embarrassed as you do what is best for your friend, despite what others think. But getting her to Jesus is what counts. Don't let anything stop you.

· ·

Lord, give me wisdom to know how best to serve
my friend in a way that brings her to You. Amen.

DETERMINED TO DO GOOD

*And let us not grow weary of doing good, for in due
season we will reap, if we do not give up. So then, as
we have opportunity, let us do good to everyone, and
especially to those who are of the household of faith.*

GALATIANS 6:9–10 ESV

How we treat others is an indication of how seriously we take
our love for the Lord. Jesus told us that to love "our neighbor
as ourselves" images our surrendered love for God (Matthew
22:38–39). The integrity of our friendships matters.

The apostle Paul, under divine inspiration, wrote that we
should not give up doing what is good to everyone. Today, be
determined to bless your friends, speak truthfully with them,
and point them to Christ. Friendship is a reflection of our
biblical understanding. Your friends need you.

. . . .

*Father God, I love You, and so I make a deliberate
choice to love others. In Jesus' name. Amen.*

FOR HER BENEFIT

No one has greater love [no one has shown stronger affection]
than to lay down (give up) his own life for his friends.
JOHN 15:13 AMPC

Self-awareness is an attribute that babies must develop, but self-comfort is there right from the start! Ask any mom of a newborn.

As we grow up, we begin to understand that it is okay, even good, to subordinate our needs for those of others. That is the underlying principle when we teach children to "share" toys. I can sacrifice what I want so someone else can benefit.

The most powerful kind of sacrifice a friend can make is to give her life for the other. Few of us will be called on to take a bullet for our bestie, but what about sacrificing in some other small way for her good?

. . . .

Lord Jesus, You laid down Your life for
me. Thank You for Your sacrifice. Amen.

ENERGY NEEDED

But those who wait on the Lord shall renew their strength;
they shall mount up with wings like eagles, they shall
run and not be weary, they shall walk and not faint.

ISAIAH 40:31 NKJV

Sometimes, a lack of emotional energy can deplete a friendship of its zest. You both still care about the other's life and family and still have some interests and philosophies in common, but because of a life season or busyness or whatever, you're lacking the energy to invest.

Today's verse speaks to spiritual needs and not to friendship, but the principle of bringing everything to the Lord applies to *everything*. If your friendship is one that will help you live a better, God-glorifying life, ask Him to renew it with His energy.

* *

Father, You give life to all things. Today,
I ask that You would imbue new energy to
this good friendship. In Jesus' name. Amen.

FEASTING IN THE HEART

All the days of the desponding and afflicted are made evil [by anxious thoughts and forebodings], but he who has a glad heart has a continual feast [regardless of circumstances].
PROVERBS 15:15 AMPC

A woman who delights in culinary things may express her friendship to you in gifts of a meal at her house or some pastry to have with your coffee in the morning. Being with her is a continual feast, literally.

Even if you aren't a proficient chef, you can give your friends ongoing delight by your glad heart. Positivity is one of the rare gifts of friendship that is much needed today. We all love to be in the presence of someone who has a glad heart. Try it.

* *

Dear God, thank You for the hope I have in You; help me to show that in a glad heart and attitude today. Amen.

MY RIGHTS OR MY FORBEARANCE

Bearing with one another and making
allowances because you love one another.
EPHESIANS 4:2 AMPC

"Standing up for my rights" is a phrase that has probably been heard, in some variation of wording, down through time. When we perceive an obstacle to our preferred way of doing things or a hint that our freedom of expression may be limited (the thermostat, the remote, preference of vacation time, etc.), we become militant in our crusade for our rights.

The Bible speaks little of rights but much of responsibility and of forbearance. These are not the happiest of words for a society that values individuality, but biblical nonetheless.

To be a true friend, one must follow the Bible's teaching and "make allowances" for the behavioral quirks and irritating actions of others because we love them.

* *

Lord of all, I ask today that You would give me the
spiritual grace to forbear with my friends. Amen.

FORGIVING FRIENDSHIP

*Be kind to one another, tenderhearted, forgiving
one another, as God in Christ forgave you.*
EPHESIANS 4:32 ESV

Whenever the theme of forgiveness is broached in a church
service or conference session, there is inevitably much interest
and much angst. Undoubtedly, forgiveness touches all of us at
the deepest level. We all need to be forgiven, and we all need
to forgive someone. All of us have been wronged by another.
And being willing to forgive and understanding how to do it
biblically are very important.

If you are going to be a good friend, you need to be a
forgiving friend. There is no getting around the fact that others
will sometimes offend and insult and irritate us. Sometimes,
they wound us. But, because Christ forgave us, we can choose
to forgive them.

. . . .

*Father God, You forgave us through Christ. I ask You
to help me forgive my offenders. In Jesus' name. Amen.*

HOPE FOR WOMANHOOD
CULTIVATE AN AGELESS SOUL

But let your adorning be the hidden person of the heart with the imperishable beauty of a gentle and quiet spirit, which in God's sight is very precious.

1 PETER 3:4 ESV

Beauty is only skin-deep.

Most of us have heard that saying. But, biblically, it's not true.

Oh, we know what is meant is that outer beauty is shallow and inner qualities matter more. But, if we take God's Word literally, the soul can actually be beautiful. The inner person of a woman who has cultivated and deliberately showcased a gentle and quiet spirit is agelessly beautiful. It is, in a very real sense, an eternal beauty, for our surrender to Christ is completed there.

· ·

Creator God, create in me an ageless beauty as I allow Your Spirit to help me have a gentle and quiet spirit. In Jesus' name. Amen.

NO ABUSE

"Holy, holy, holy is the LORD of hosts;
the whole earth is full of His glory!"
ISAIAH 6:3 NKJV

Being more delicate in physical structure because we are made for childbearing and being more sensitive in emotional ways because we are designed for relationship and nurture, women have often been abused down through time. It was rather easy for a bad man to gain control over a woman for the simple reason that he could overpower her in various ways.

But God is absolutely holy, and there is no flaw in His character; because of that, we can trust Him, and we can trust the men who truly follow Him. Holiness denotes respect for others. Learn to look for the indicators of personal holiness in the men who admire your beauty.

. . . .

Lord, I am glad that You are perfectly holy, for
that means You are perfectly trustworthy. Amen.

WHAT YOU NEED

*Now the young woman pleased him, and she
obtained his favor; so he readily gave beauty
preparations to her, besides her allowance.*

ESTHER 2:9 NKJV

It is interesting that the Bible tells us that Hegai, the steward over the Persian king's harem, was very generous with the young Esther who was preparing for her audition with the king. And because Esther was a young woman who feared God, no doubt her manner was pleasant, and she attracted his favor.

As we follow God, we need not fear that He will provide what we need. Does this mean we will have lavish resources with which to pamper ourselves foolishly? No, but we will be able to live a life that brings glory to Him with whatever is on hand.

. . . .

*Father God, I trust You with the provisions I
need to care for the body You've given me. Amen.*

FIRST GAZE

*My frame was not hidden from You when I was
being formed in secret [and] intricately and curiously
wrought [as if embroidered with various colors] in
the depths of the earth [a region of darkness and
mystery]. Your eyes saw my unformed substance.*
PSALM 139:15–16 AMPC

Most expectant mothers cherish the images from their
sonogram appointment—their first look at the child inside,
waiting to be born. But the Bible tells us that Someone has
already seen that little one. The first eyes to behold any of us
were His.

As women, we are intensely aware that eyes constantly
notice us, look at us, evaluate us. But we must remember that the
first gaze upon us was His, a Father who loves us, His creation.

* *

*Father in heaven, help me to remember today that Your
gaze was the first and is the most important. Amen.*

WHY IS NAKEDNESS A BIG DEAL?

Women should adorn themselves in respectable
apparel, with modesty and self-control.
1 TIMOTHY 2:9 ESV

The only context in the Bible in which nakedness is expressed in a positive manner is before sin entered the world, when the first man and first woman were naked and unashamed. After they sinned, they tried to cover themselves, understanding that even their bodies were somehow implicated in this need for redemption.

God affirmed their desire for clothing by making them coats that covered more of their bodies than their fig-leaf aprons. And He instituted laws designed to protect the vulnerability of the naked body. Women are specifically instructed to guard their bodies because the power of the female form is great. When we understand that God does all things for our good, we can see modesty as a beauty tool, not as a hindrance.

* *

Dear God, I ask that You would give me wisdom
as I choose my clothing today. Amen.

YOUR BEAUTY, HIS SIGNATURE

*For you formed my inward parts; you knitted
me together in my mother's womb. I praise you,
for I am fearfully and wonderfully made.*

PSALM 139:13–14 ESV

An original, signed painting by one of the great masters is incredibly valuable. Collectors pay handsomely to obtain one. Museums go to great lengths to add to their collections. The kind of image varies in these classic pieces; it's the name on them that makes them valuable.

And so it is with us and our physical beauty. We bear the signature of the Artist. He formed us and put us together, sculpting us into a masterpiece of His creation. We are each unique. We are each valuable. Comparing ourselves with other works of art is useless since every creation is one-of-a-kind. Your place is secure in His collection.

. . . .

*Lord God, I want to reflect You well with the
beauty You've given me. In Jesus' name. Amen.*

REDEEMED FLAWS

But the question really is this: "Who are you, a man,
to make any such reply to God?" When a craftsman
makes anything he doesn't expect it to turn round
and say, 'Why did you make me like this?' "
ROMANS 9:20 PHILLIPS

Every woman has them. Flaws. Facial flaws. Figure flaws.
Beauty flaws.

When we look at ourselves in the mirror, we usually dismiss
the good points and focus on the problems. We can't even seem
to see what's right because we are so ashamed of what's wrong.

God, our Creator, wants us to know that there is hope for
our beauty because He created it. The flaws that are a result
of fallenness cannot annihilate His good design. We may
not see the perfection of us until we get to heaven, but we
must believe it is there!

. . . .

Designer God, I know You have made me and that my
flaws will be redeemed someday in Your presence. Amen.

THE WAY WE'RE MADE

That the younger women may learn to love their husbands
and their children, to be sensible and chaste, home-lovers,
kind-hearted and willing to adapt themselves to their
husbands—a good advertisement for the Christian faith.

TITUS 2:4–5 PHILLIPS

It is a good thing for us to remind ourselves of what the Bible says and to seek to understand how we can apply it today.

Most women would agree that part of the beauty of womanhood is the joy of nurturing others, and that often it happens in a home setting. Whether women are actually biological mothers or not, they still possess maternal qualities that find delight in caring for others. We must never forget this important distinctive of womanhood; it's a way we reflect our Creator.

. . . .

O God, You have created me to care for and
nurture others. Help me do it well. Amen.

WORTHY AND REDEEMED

For you must realise all the time that you have been
"ransomed". . .not with some money payment of
transient value, but by the costly shedding of blood.
1 PETER 1:18 PHILLIPS

Comparing ourselves to one another and guesstimating our worth are activities we engage in from girlhood. We easily fall into the idea that those who have a certain waist circumference or certain hair color or brand-name clothing or whatever are worth more. It makes sense to our childly minds—she is prettier than me; she has nicer shoes, therefore, she is more important.

God has a very different scale for determining our worth.

1. Our creation—He made us: He only makes good things.
2. Our redemption—He gave the costly gift of His Son.

Both of these reasons say we are of ultimate worth to Him.

. . . .

Heavenly Father, I look to You to
determine my value today. Amen.

A GREAT IDEA

Now the Lord God said, It is not good (sufficient,
satisfactory) that the man should be alone; I will make
him a helper (suitable, adapted, complementary) for him.
GENESIS 2:18 AMPC

Neither was man created on account of or for the benefit of
woman, but woman on account of and for the benefit of man.
1 CORINTHIANS 11:9 AMPC

God wanted to create beings who would choose to be in relationship with Him. And He wanted to create beings who would be in relationship with one another.

So He created two reflections of His image and gave them personal choice. He created Eve from Adam's rib—a metaphor for how close they should be and an indication that she was made to make human relationship possible. This does not mean that women who are not married are devoid of meaning but rather gives us understanding that we need one another.

* *

Heavenly Creator, thank You for creating relationships
and most of all, for relationship with You. Amen.

NOT TEMPORARY

*He has made everything beautiful in its time. He also has
planted eternity in men's hearts and minds [a divinely
implanted sense of a purpose working through the ages
which nothing under the sun but God alone can satisfy].*
ECCLESIASTES 3:11 AMPC

So many things about our lives as women are temporary
and fleeting: our youth, our beauty, our babies, our health,
our careers, even sometimes our marriages when death or
abandonment makes us widows prematurely.

But, if we belong to Him, our identity as daughters of God
is eternal. We have that knowledge that He is working out His
purpose in us throughout the ages.

Our faces may show wrinkles, our children may grow up
and leave, our bodies may stop working correctly, our ability
to work and have hobbies may diminish. But our ability to "be"
in God never ends.

*O Lord, thank You for the hope of eternity
where my purpose in You is secure. Amen.*

HOPE FOR A GOOD REPUTATION
TRUTH SEEKING AND SPEAKING

I have chosen the way of faithfulness;
I set your rules before me.
PSALM 119:30 ESV

Having a good reputation matters. And the way we interact with others around us is what builds our reputation.

Being a truth speaker can have both positive and negative results. Standing for what is right, morally and ethically, is foundational for a healthy society. But, on the other hand, many citizens in our society do not appreciate having their consciences alerted.

God's Word is ultimate Truth. It is the standard by which we will be judged and the final arbiter of our decisions and behavior. Having a reputation as a truth-seeker and truth-speaker points to a life that seeks Him.

. . . .

Lord, I want my life reputation to be one that honors
Your ultimate Truth. Give me the desire to seek it
and the wisdom to speak it. In Jesus' name. Amen.

KNOWN FOR SMILING

A glad heart makes a cheerful face, but by
sorrow of heart the spirit is crushed.
PROVERBS 15:13 ESV

A great reputation to have is that of a smiling person. Mark Twain is credited with saying "Wrinkles should merely indicate where the smiles have been." And that would be a pretty great way to welcome wrinkles if we must have them.

There is much to frown about, for sure. The daily news leaves us aghast, the weather may be inclement, our health may not be great, and our family may be experiencing difficulties.

But we don't smile because we have no problems; we smile in spite of them. We need to remind ourselves that we are representatives of Jesus, and we can smile because He is always in control.

• •

Dear Lord, let me be known as a woman
who smiles in every season. Amen.

BEING A HELPER

"But a certain Samaritan, as he journeyed, came where he was. And when he saw him, he had compassion. So he went to him and bandaged his wounds, pouring on oil and wine; and he set him on his own animal, brought him to an inn, and took care of him. On the next day, when he departed, he took out two denarii, gave them to the innkeeper, and said to him, 'Take care of him; and whatever more you spend, when I come again, I will repay you.'"
LUKE 10:32–35 NKJV

A great reputation is that of helpfulness. We only know about the Good Samaritan because Jesus told the story. But quietly, without fanfare, the Good Samaritan helped a stranger. We can do the same.

. . . .

Jesus, You helped others in Your earthly ministry. Help me to follow Your example. Amen.

SHARING LIFE WITH OTHERS

"And when she has found it, she calls together her
friends and neighbors, saying, 'Rejoice with me,
for I have found the coin that I had lost.' "

LUKE 15:9 ESV

Friendliness is one of those reputations that most of us would like to claim. Few of us want to be known as the neighborhood grump or the mean lady next door.

One of the ways to be friendly is to invite the people around you into your life in appropriate ways. Some families host block parties or neighborhood barbecues. The lady in the parable Jesus told invited her friends to a celebration. She let them share in her joy. When we invite others into the moments of our lives, we create friendships.

. . . .

Father in heaven, help me to be willing to share
my life in good ways with others around me so
that I can have a reputation of friendliness. Amen.

HONORING OTHERS

Love one another with brotherly affection.
Outdo one another in showing honor.
ROMANS 12:10 ESV

Being a person who respects others is a worthwhile reputation.

There are many things that pull at the fabric of society; lack of respect is one of them. When people neglect or refuse to respect one another because of differences of background, opinion, ethnicity, or other reasons, the culture deteriorates. Genuine respect fosters civil behavior and logical conversations and compromise on issues that matter to all.

You can be a woman who is known for her respect for others. Your friends and acquaintances and neighbors should have no doubt that you will honor them as human beings even if you don't agree on every point of life. Jesus honored people; we should do the same.

* *

Father God, remind me that every single person is a reflection of Your image; help me honor everyone. Amen.

SHOWING COMPASSION

*To sum up, you should all be of one mind living like brothers
with true love and sympathy for each other, generous and
courteous at all times. Never pay back a bad turn with
a bad turn or an insult with another insult, but on the
contrary pay back with good. For this is your calling—to
do good and one day to inherit all the goodness of God.*

1 PETER 3:8–9 PHILLIPS

We are tempted to think that to show compassion we must donate
time at the food bank or at the downtown mission for the homeless
or as a volunteer at the local Christian pregnancy center.

Yet compassion can also be offering a ride to someone whose
car is in repair or taking a meal to a church family experiencing
illness or helping a young mom with her children.

Compassion is doing what you can for those in need.

. . . .

*Lord, give me eyes to see ways to show
compassion. In Jesus' name. Amen.*

ALWAYS THE SAME

But You remain the same,
and Your years shall have no end.
PSALM 102:27 AMPC

God is the only entity in the universe who is always exactly the same. He has the supernatural divine quality of never changing. We are constantly changing in big and little ways; some are barely perceptible to others while some are the first thing people notice.

Treating others the same whenever we see them is a wonderful reputation. If a woman is moody—sometimes cheerful and talkative and then sometimes withdrawn and quiet—others will never quite know how they should approach her. The people we love to be around always greet us, make us feel important, and show by their smiles that they are glad to see us. Let's strive for that reputation.

* *

O God, I'm glad You don't change. Help me
to be consistent in treating others well. Amen.

UNCOMMON HONESTY

Therefore, having put away falsehood, let each
one of you speak the truth with his neighbor,
for we are members one of another.

EPHESIANS 4:25 ESV

The old saying goes that "Honesty is the best policy." And a reputation of honest dealing is one to be prized.

In our grandparents' day, a man's word was solid. And honesty was the finest commodity for a business.

While honesty is still valued and expressed today in our culture, a lack of public recognition of moral code like the Ten Commandments has led to greater dishonesty in general, even in ways that many consider common for everyone.

If you can be known as a woman who always tells the truth, you will have a reputation worth keeping.

* *

Dear Lord, prick my conscience when I get near to shading
the truth, and help me value honesty. In Jesus' name. Amen.

DEVOTED TO MINISTRY

*This is how one should regard us, as servants
of Christ and stewards of the mysteries of God.*
1 CORINTHIANS 4:1 ESV

Ministry is not only done in a church; it is accomplished anywhere we serve another in need. Ministry therefore can happen at a school meeting, in a crowded grocery store, standing in line at the post office, and in many other places.

There are specific types of ministry, of course. Some women minister as nurses in a hospital. Some women serve in ministry as teachers to small children. Some women care for elderly parents or volunteer at the local assisted-living facility or work in the church nursery. Whatever your ministry, do it with a cheerful heart and a focus on loving Him and others.

* *

*Dear God, thank You for sending Jesus as the great
example of ministry. I want to be like Him. Amen.*

85

WORSHIP WITH JOY

Lift up your hands to the holy place and bless the LORD!
PSALM 134:2 ESV

In developing your reputation, don't forget about worship.

A woman who worships is a woman who has her priorities right. Worship means we understand who is truly worthy, and we offer Him the adoration of our hearts and the obedience of our lives. Worship is a way to give public voice to the thankfulness we should express because of His goodness to us in sending His Son. Worship tells others that we keep first things first.

Being known in your church as a woman who worships is one of the greatest compliments you could receive. Never be ashamed to lift your hands toward the Lord and give Him honor.

. . . .

Father in heaven, You alone deserve my worship.
I want to be known as a worshipper of You. Amen.

HOPE FOR EVERYDAY LIFE
ANOTHER MORNING SUN

The sun also rises and the sun goes down,
and hastens to the place where it rises.
ECCLESIASTES 1:5 AMPC

Everyday life begins and ends with the sun, in a manner of speaking. Of course, on some days, the sun isn't visible where we are—hidden behind clouds or obscured by inclement weather. But the dawning of a new day is a natural reset button that God built into our world. This is one of the challenges for those who work the night shift; their center of refocus is gone because they work through the hours when our minds were meant to defragment and be restored.

Yesterday may have been horrible. And its pain may still be with you. But God has created today to help you with yesterday. And the shining of the sun is His reminder.

. . . .

Creator God, thank You for the sun and
its brilliant way of reminding me. Amen.

MAKE SOME MUSIC

Give thanks to the Lord with the lyre; sing
praises to Him with the harp of ten strings.
PSALM 33:2 AMPC

Stringed instruments were common in the days when the Bible was written. Just like in Appalachia, there was, no doubt, a great assortment of musical items made with strings. Who was the first person to discover that blowing into a hollow tube, plucking a taut string, or hitting a stretched piece of skin with a mallet would make music? Someone did, and music-making has been part of human life ever since.

When you get up tomorrow, invest in your everyday life by turning on uplifting, Christ-centered music to remind you that there is hope and joy for your next twenty-four hours.

* *

Lord, You created music for our enjoyment and
for Your glory. Thank You for this rich gift. Amen.

FRESH FROM HIS HAND

*They gathered it every morning, each as much
as he needed, for when the sun became hot it
melted. . . . The house of Israel called the bread
manna; it was like coriander seed, white, and
it tasted like wafers made with honey.*

EXODUS 16:21, 31 AMPC

Do you have a morning ritual? Most of us do. We roll out of
bed after turning off the alarm and shuffle to the bathroom or
to the kitchen. For many of us, the morning routine probably
involves pouring a cup of coffee from the coffeepot or brewing
an individual cup. Some add cream, some add sugar, and a few
hearty souls drink it black.

Our morning refreshment surely doesn't compare to the
manna God gave to the ancient Hebrews. But every good thing
in our morning should remind us again that blessings come
from His hand, fresh every day.

• •

*O God, I delight in Your daily provisions for
me, even down to my cup of coffee. Amen.*

DIVINE BREATH

The Spirit of God has made me, and the
breath of the Almighty gives me life.
JOB 33:4 ESV

If you've ever had to have your oxygen level checked for medical reasons, you know that there is a healthy percentage at which it should be detectable in your bloodstream. The body needs the energy from oxygen in order to live.

The Bible tells us that God breathed living air through His Spirit into Adam's lungs, and symbolically every human being since has been a recipient of that divine breath.

Job tells us that our daily oxygen comes from the Almighty. It is one of His daily gifts and a reason that we can have hope. He is the life giver.

. . . .

Jehovah God, thank You for breath and life.
I praise You for Your marvelous creation. Amen.

90

HEALTHY ROUTINE

Everyone also to whom God has given wealth and
possessions and power to enjoy them, and to accept
his lot and rejoice in his toil—this is the gift of God.
ECCLESIASTES 5:19 ESV

Often we grow bored with routine, of doing the same things over and over, of going on monotonously with the repeated motions of everyday life.

But routine is also one of God's gifts that reminds us we have hope in the everyday. Routine symbolizes that we have stability in life and some measure of safety as well as the means to do the same thing tomorrow that we did today.

Routine is healthy for our minds and for our budgets, keeping us from random decisions and from unwise spending and keeping us steady in the channel of life.

. . . .

Creator God, thank You for giving me the resources
to have a daily routine. I'm grateful. Amen.

ADEQUATE CLOSETS

"And why do you worry about clothes? Consider how the wild flowers grow. They neither work nor weave, but I tell you that even Solomon in all his glory was never arrayed like one of these! Now if God so clothes the flowers of the field, which are alive today and burnt in the stove tomorrow, is he not much more likely to clothe you, you 'little-faiths'?"
MATTHEW 6:28–30 PHILLIPS

Having a closet filled with beautiful clothing is the dream of many women, but we are not promised a lavish wardrobe. We are, however, promised that God will take care of this need in greater measure than He even does the flowers of the field. This is the assurance we have every morning as our feet hit the floor.

. . . .

O God, thank You for taking care of my clothing needs. My closet is Your space. Amen.

PERFECT SENSES

And the LORD said to him, Who hath made
man's mouth? Or who maketh the dumb, or deaf,
or the seeing, or the blind? Have not I, the LORD?
EXODUS 4:11 KJV

As we rise every morning to face a new hope, an important one is the often-discounted joy of having five senses—seeing, hearing, tasting, smelling, and touching. These ways in which we interact with the world around us remind us that our God wants us to take pleasure both in nature and in other human beings.

When a physical sense is lost because of an accident or genetic abnormality, the others become heightened to help make up the difference. Considering the genius of our Creator, we should start each new day in awe of our senses that connect us to the world and to each other.

. . . .

Thank You, God, for making ears, eyes, nose, mouth,
and skin. Your goodness gives me hope. Amen.

LUXURY OF HOME

Like a bird that wanders from her nest,
so is a man who strays from his home.
PROVERBS 27:8 AMPC

They say there's no place like it, and most of us would agree. No matter how much we wish to update it or need to clean it and wish to sell it, there is no other place quite like the place we call home.

Some of us live in apartments and some in framed houses, some in modular or mobile homes, and some in condos or townhouses. Some of us own our homes, and some of us rent or share living space with relatives. But all of us value the sacred space where we can relax and be refreshed. And the luxury of a home spot is one we often forget.

. . . .

Lord Jesus, You didn't have a home on earth,
but You have promised that You will share Yours
with me in heaven. Thank You. Amen.

94

STEADFAST SEASONS

He changes the times and the seasons; He removes
kings and sets up kings. He gives wisdom to the wise
and knowledge to those who have understanding!
DANIEL 2:21 AMPC

One of the greatest reminders that we have hope is the changing of the seasons.

After the Great Flood, God promised Noah that the springtime and harvest and summer and winter would not perish as long as the earth remained (Genesis 8:22). We may rest in that fact while reveling in the fiery colors of fall, the tranquility of winter, the green flurry of spring, and the bright warmth of summer. The seasons are set into the cycle of earth which He upholds.

Whatever the season outside your window today, find hope in the fact that it has appeared like clockwork, on His schedule.

. . . .

God of heaven, the seasons remind me of Your steadfast
truth and unfailing promises. Thank you for hope. Amen.

MIND KEEPING

For God did not give us a spirit of timidity (of cowardice, of craven and cringing and fawning fear), but [He has given us a spirit] of power and of love and of calm and well-balanced mind and discipline and self-control.

2 TIMOTHY 1:7 AMPC

God has limited His power to allow us freedom of choice. This includes the kinds of input we give our minds. He instructs us about what is best, and He gives us the alarms of conscience and the Holy Spirit. And He promises that if we center our minds on His thoughts, He will keep us balanced and safe. We will have to do our part in saying no to anxiety and yes to trust.

The fact that He watches over our minds gives us hope for the days ahead.

* *

Dear God, please keep my mind safe from the devil's attacks today. In Jesus' name. Amen.

HOPE FOR MARRIAGE
GOOD COMPANIONS

Then the LORD God said, "It is not good that the man
should be alone; I will make him a helper fit for him."
GENESIS 2:18 ESV

Two are better than one, because they have a good
reward for their toil. For if they fall, one will lift
up his fellow. But woe to him who is alone when
he falls and has not another to lift him up!
ECCLESIASTES 4:9–10 ESV

You don't often hear people cite companionship as a reason for marriage, but actually it is a biblical reason. Now, theologically, it is only one component of what we understand to be God's plan for marriage with other reasons being the completion of God's image in human form, earthly procreation, symbolism of Christ and the Church, etc. But "being alone" was "not good" in the Creator's eyes.

Creator God, I give You thanks for the companionship
You created in marriage. Amen.

LIVE IT OUT

*In the same spirit you married women should adapt
yourselves to your husbands, so that even if they do
not obey the Word of God they may be won to God
without any word being spoken, simply by seeing the
pure and reverent behaviour of you, their wives.*

1 PETER 3:1 PHILLIPS

There are few things more emotionally painful than continual
disagreement with someone you love. A believing woman who
finds herself married to an unbelieving man (for whatever
reason) will experience isolation, longing, and sadness.

Scripture addresses this problem, telling wives to exhibit
the biblical behavior that God expects from them, which will, in
turn, have a life-changing effect on their husbands. The living
Word, put into skin through human action, is always powerful.

Don't be discouraged; live it out.

*Heavenly Father, prompt me through Your Spirit to
live in ways that will point my husband to You. Amen.*

USE BUILDING WORDS

Let no corrupting talk come out of your mouths,
but only such as is good for building up, as fits the
occasion, that it may give grace to those who hear.

EPHESIANS 4:29 ESV

Probably the single most important way we can invest in and improve our marriages is by guarding the way we talk to our husbands. Our words can either build up or tear down— romance, his worth in his own eyes, his desire to show affection, and our ability to partner together in parenting, ministry, and everyday life.

The teaching here to the church at Ephesus is generally used in terms of church relationships, but why shouldn't it be applicable to husbands and wives, who are also members of the Body? If we try to "edify" or build up our husbands today, who knows what amazing results there would be!

· ·

Lord God, I want to build up my husband
today with my words. Give me courage. Amen.

A MATTER OF BALANCE

Fathers, do not provoke your children to anger, but bring them up in the discipline and instruction of the Lord.
EPHESIANS 6:4 ESV

Agreeing with your husband on parenting techniques, discipline in particular, can be a challenge in marriage. Sometimes, there are differing degrees of law and grace in the mix. One parent will more often lean toward firmness, and one will feel a bit more sympathy. The balance is that, together, you can have the right approach. Learn from each other. Discuss it together. But try never to object to or question your husband while he is disciplining one of your children. And if he is wrong, either too strict or too lax, ask God to work on his heart.

. . . .

God, today give my husband the wisdom he needs to be a good dad to our children. Amen.

FUN HOURS

"When a man is newly married, he shall not go out with the army or be liable for any other public duty. He shall be free at home one year to be happy with his wife whom he has taken."

DEUTERONOMY 24:5 ESV

In ancient Israel, God instituted special exemptions for a newly married man. He was to be free in many ways to get to know his wife and "to be happy" with her at home.

Time together is very important. In our romance and sex-saturated culture, we might not put priority on the aspect of being friends—taking walks, playing games, hiking, riding bikes, getting ice cream, exploring new coffee shops, etc. But spending fun hours as a couple will reap great dividends.

. . . .

Lord, I want to have the kind of attitude that will prompt my husband to want to spend time with me. Amen.

DON'T CONFUSE THE TWO

*Be eager and strive earnestly to guard and keep
the harmony and oneness of [and produced
by] the Spirit in the binding power of peace.*
EPHESIANS 4:3 AMPC

We often confuse uniformity with unity and sameness with oneness.

In marriage, it is impossible to have uniformity and sameness. There are two fundamentally opposite people involved—a man and a woman, a male and a female. And beyond that, there are two distinct personalities and sets of preferences as well as two different backgrounds and experiences.

We can have unity by agreeing to live in harmony and to make our differences work for us. We can have oneness by acknowledging that we are one flesh in God's covenant of marriage and choose to move forward in life as one household of faith.

. . . .

*Father, You are the Creator of marriage.
Make us one in You. In Jesus' name. Amen.*

A SYMBOL OF ROMANCE

Let him kiss me with the kisses of his mouth!
SONG OF SOLOMON 1:2 ESV

A kiss has long been in our American culture the symbol of deep romantic attraction—in literature and film, theater and song. Little children giggle at the brightness of the bridal kiss. Young girls shyly gaze with longing, hoping for their own magical romance. Young men imagine the thrill of their sweetheart's lips.

In the daily life of marriage, we sometimes forget to kiss. Though we may have times of marital intimacy, it may not include affection. Strange, isn't it?

Women love it when men lead. God designed it that way. But we can do all we can to invite our husbands to enjoy the sweet pleasure of a kiss. Give it your best!

• •

God, You invented romance because You invented marriage.
Draw my husband toward me today in romance. Amen.

A MATTER OF RESPECT

However, let each one of you love his wife as himself,
and let the wife see that she respects her husband.
EPHESIANS 5:33 ESV

From childhood to manhood, men thrive on respect. Their childhood dreams center on being someone who, in their minds, is respected. As adolescents, many engage in sports as their chief way of seeking respect; some prefer more artistic venues, but they still bring a male approach to it, a drive to succeed and be respected for it. This differs from women who, with few exceptions, desire more to be respected for who we are than for what we do.

As adult men, our husbands derive respect, not only from their professions, trades, or ministry but also from their relationship with their wives. When we admire them, ask their advice, honor their opinions, and build them up to others, everyone wins.

. . . .

Dear Lord, today, with Your help, I will find
ways to show respect to my husband. Amen.

BONDED THROUGH PRAYER

Don't worry over anything whatever; tell God every detail of your needs in earnest and thankful prayer, and the peace of God which transcends human understanding, will keep constant guard over your hearts and minds as they rest in Christ Jesus.
PHILIPPIANS 4:6–7 PHILLIPS

Praying together as a husband and wife is one of the most powerful bonding agents at our disposal. Like the construction of a triangle, as husband in one corner and wife in the other corner draw closer to God at the top, they draw closer to each other. *That* is an appropriate kind of love triangle!

When a wife tries to nag her husband into prayer time to get close to him, it rather defeats the purpose. So pray that God will change his mind about praying with you!

O Lord, please put in my husband's heart a desire to pray with me. In Jesus' name. Amen.

BONDING THROUGH FORGIVING

*"And whenever you stand praying, you must forgive
anything that you are holding against anyone else,
and your Heavenly Father will forgive you your sins."*

MARK 11:25-26 PHILLIPS

Ruth Bell Graham is quoted as saying, "A happy marriage is the union of two good forgivers."

Demanding our rights, expecting the other person to come our way first, refusing to overlook little things, keeping a list of faults and offenses—all of these things will destroy a marriage. The only way to have a happy marriage with our husbands is to be quick to forgive.

Forgiveness doesn't erase hurt or make apologies unnecessary, but it does acknowledge that we, as wives, often need forgiveness too, and this marriage is an ongoing bonding between two fallible people.

* *

*Father in heaven, thank You for forgiving me through
my belief in Christ; help me extend forgiveness to my
husband whenever he needs it. In Jesus' name. Amen.*

HOPE FOR GIFTS

CONTRIBUTE WHAT YOU CAN

Everyone to whom much was given, of him much
will be required, and from him to whom they
entrusted much, they will demand the more.

LUKE 12:48 ESV

When we were little, we might have heard someone say, "God has a wonderful plan for your life."

Every single person was designed to contribute beautifully to the earthly template of existence. Some people cannot use their gifts because of the tragedy of genetic abnormality or devastating injury, and some cannot contribute because their very lives were taken through abortion.

But on those who are living and well is the responsibility to use our gifts well for the glory of our Creator and the good of others.

. . . .

I trust You today, Lord, to come alongside me as
I use the gifts You've ordained me to have. Amen.

FIND YOUR GIFTS

*She seeks wool and flax, and works with willing
hands. . . . She considers a field and buys it; with
the fruit of her hands she plants a vineyard. . . . She
puts her hands to the distaff, and her hands hold the
spindle. . . . She makes linen garments and sells them.*
PROVERBS 31:13, 16, 19, 24 ESV

In looking at the woman described in Proverbs 31, we can discover that she was a woman who used her personal abilities for the good of others and, ultimately, for the glory of God.

You may not be a seamstress or a realtor or a manufacturer of cloth or a clothing designer as she is described in these verses, but you do have abilities and inclinations toward creativity. Find out what they are and how you can use them in righteous ways.

* *

*Dear God, I bring to You my abilities.
Bless them as I use them for You. Amen.*

USE IT FOR GOD

But the midwives feared God and did not do as the king
of Egypt commanded them, but let the male children
live. . . . So God dealt well with the midwives. And the
people multiplied and grew very strong. And because
the midwives feared God, he gave them families.
EXODUS 1:17, 20–21 ESV

In the time when God's people were in captivity in Egypt,
there were two very busy Hebrew midwives—Shiphrah and
Puah. They dared to defy Pharoah's decree about killing the
Hebrew baby boys. And because of that, God blessed them
and gave them their own families.

These women used their abilities to bless God's people and
to protect life and to advance God's plans. We may use their
example to encourage us to do the same.

* *

God of all, may my stewardship of my
abilities fulfill Your purposes. Amen.

NEVER TOO OLD

And there was a prophetess, Anna, the daughter of Phanuel, of the tribe of Asher. She was advanced in years, having lived with her husband seven years from when she was a virgin, and then as a widow until she was eighty-four. She did not depart from the temple, worshiping with fasting and prayer night and day. And coming up at that very hour she began to give thanks to God and to speak of him to all who were waiting for the redemption of Jerusalem.
LUKE 2:36–38 ESV

If you are a widow or in your later years, don't imagine that the days of using your gifts are over. Anna blessed a young mother and gave witness to the truth of God's promise when she was way into retirement age. You can too.

· ·

O Lord, thank You that You will continue to use me for as long as I allow You to do so. Amen.

NEVER IN CONFLICT

He began to speak boldly in the synagogue, but when
Priscilla and Aquila heard him, they took him aside
and explained to him the way of God more accurately.
ACTS 18:26 ESV

Greet Prisca and Aquila, my fellow workers in Christ Jesus.
ROMANS 16:3 ESV

Our God-given gifts and abilities are to be used with knowledge of God's Word and in tandem with the life and family He has given us. The use of God's gifts never conflicts with the truth of His Word and is always in harmony with our surrender to His will.

The woman, Priscilla or Prisca, used her teaching skills alongside her husband and was commended by the apostle Paul. She models the concept of harmony of scripture and gift.

• •

I need discernment, Lord, as a I seek to understand
how You want me to use my gifts. Amen.

NO HIDING ALLOWED

*To one he gave five talents, to another two, to another
one, to each according to his ability. Then he went
away. He who had received the five talents went at once
and traded with them, and he made five talents more.
So also he who had the two talents made two talents
more. But he who had received the one talent went and
dug in the ground and hid his master's money.*
MATTHEW 25:15–18 ESV

To us, it seems unfair that one servant was given more than
another, but we must leave that to God. They are His resources
after all. And it is important to note that the servant who was
given one didn't even use that one! What would he have done
if he'd been given more?

Be courageous, pray for God's help, and then use your
abilities!

*Lord Jesus, today I will not hide my
gift but use it in Your name. Amen.*

PAY OFF DEBTS AT HOME

As she poured they brought the vessels to her. When the
vessels were full, she said to her son, "Bring me another
vessel." And he said to her, "There is not another."
Then the oil stopped flowing. She came and told the
man of God, and he said, "Go, sell the oil and pay your
debts, and you and your sons can live on the rest."
2 KINGS 4:5–7 ESV

Perhaps hers was the first home-based business. She sought
advice from the prophet. If you are thinking of starting a
home-based business to help out your family and to use your
entrepreneurial and creative abilities, remember to ask God
for wisdom and to consult godly people for counsel. When we
have His blessing, we avoid much trouble.

· ·

Dear Lord, guide my thoughts and grant me discernment
as I think about starting a home-based business. Amen.

WORK AND WORSHIP

We spent some days in Philippi and on the Sabbath day we went out of the city gate to the riverside, where we supposed there was a place for prayer. There we sat down and spoke to the women who had assembled. One of our hearers was a woman named Lydia. (She came from Thyatira and was a dealer in purple-dyed cloth.) She was already a believer in God, and she opened her heart to accept Paul's words.

ACTS 16:13–14 PHILLIPS

In the days of the New Testament, one of the popular luxuries was purple cloth. Lydia, a woman of Thyatira, was a merchant dealing in the sale of purple cloth. And she also became a staunch member of the new church in Philippi.

You too can bring beauty to others and worship to God as you use your gifts, but keep worship in its proper place.

. . . .

O Lord, show me how to use my gifts and keep my priorities aligned with Your Word. Amen.

DO SOMETHING BESIDES TALK

They get into habits of slackness by being so much
in and out of other people's houses. In fact they
easily become worse than lazy, and degenerate into
gossips and busybodies with dangerous tongues.
1 TIMOTHY 5:13 PHILLIPS

This is certainly not one of the happiest nor most flattering verses in the Bible, but it is a needed admonition. We must make sure that we do not neglect to use our gifts and rather become socialites and busybodies. That can happen, even in the Church!

God gives many of us families, which are to be our first priority after Him. Then He may give us occasion to use our educational investment and personal giftedness in ways outside the home. We must not, instead, become lazy and spend our productive time talking and socially interacting, which can lead to gossip and other unhealthy tendencies.

. . . .

Lord, keep me from becoming a slacker and a talker. Amen.

USE THEM WELL

Whatever your hand finds to do, do it with all your might,
for there is no work or device or knowledge or wisdom
in Sheol (the place of the dead), where you are going.
ECCLESIASTES 9:10 AMPC

In western culture, we have things called hobbies or pastimes. They are not usually career paths or money-making ventures but rather things we do "for fun" or recreation.

The Bible tells us that whatever we do—hobby, homemaking, or business—to do it with all our might. There is no room for sloppy work or half-hearted involvement. Throw your energy into what you do because we will someday age and die and be unable to work. So we must make use of the present season God has given us.

. . . .

Lord God, thank You for the opportunities I have for rest,
recreation, and work. Help me to use them well. Amen.

HOPE FOR THE CHURCH
WORSHIP, WOMAN!

O come, let us worship and bow down, let us kneel before the Lord our Maker [in reverent praise and supplication].
PSALM 95:6 AMPC

Worship is the compass of our lives. If we want to know what we value, let's look at what we worship. In the Old Testament, as He was establishing His people, Israel, God laid down very specific laws about idolatry, likening it to spiritual adultery, an earthly reference that was easily understood. He wanted them to know that, as a loving husband desires his wife's devoted love, so He desired their hearts turned toward Him alone. These truths still apply to us today.

There is hope for a woman who worships the one true God. She may worship quietly, noisily, privately, or publicly, but her church is edified when others can observe it. And the condition of her heart is reflected in it.

• •

Jehovah God, I worship You. Reveal to me any idols that threaten my love for You. Amen.

NO DIVISIONS

God has so composed the body, giving greater honor to the part that lacked it, that there may be no division in the body, but that the members may have the same care for one another.
1 CORINTHIANS 12:24–25 ESV

The LORD hates. . .one who sows discord among brothers.
PROVERBS 6:16, 19 ESV

An old question asks "What would my church be if all its members were like me?"

God uses very strong language to describe His feelings about those who cause disruption. There is hope for the woman who refuses to verbalize negativity and criticism about church leadership or other growing Christians and instead, chooses to be part of those who support and pray for one another.

. . . .

Lord, set up an alarm in my conscience when I am about to use my tongue in sinful ways. Amen.

QUELL THE MUTINY

We ask you, brothers, to respect those who labor among you and are over you in the Lord and admonish you, and to esteem them very highly in love because of their work. Be at peace among yourselves.
1 THESSALONIANS 5:12–13 ESV

Few things will kill a church quicker than a mutiny, a coup in the congregation. When the deadly viral mix of criticism and suspicion and comparison against a pastor begins, it is almost impossible to rescue the church from an outbreak that will sicken everyone involved.

You can be a woman who has hope by maintaining your integrity in regard to your pastor. If there are legitimate concerns, there are appropriate ways to address them, but that doesn't mean standing in a huddle discussing it or texting your girlfriends about it through the week. Honor your pastor and be slow to criticize.

· ·

O God, thank You for my pastor.
Help me honor him this week. Amen.

STAY PROTECTED

Remember your leaders and superiors in authority [for it was they] who brought to you the Word of God. Observe attentively and consider their manner of living (the outcome of their well-spent lives) and imitate their faith (their conviction that God exists and is the Creator and Ruler of all things, the Provider and Bestower of eternal salvation through Christ, and their leaning of the entire human personality on God in absolute trust and confidence in His power, wisdom, and goodness).
HEBREWS 13:7 AMPC

One of the key tenets taught in the Bible is that of respect for and subordination to the proper authority, first God and then those whom He places over us in the home and in the church and in society. You can be a woman of hope by respecting the leadership in your local church and remembering that they are doing their best to watch over your soul.

- -

God, give me a submissive heart to the authority You have placed over me for my protection. Amen.

PROPER EXPRESSION

*Let Christ's teaching live in your hearts, making you rich
in the true wisdom. Teach and help one another along the
right road with your psalms and hymns and Christian
songs, singing God's praises with joyful hearts.*
COLOSSIANS 3:16 PHILLIPS

The so-called "worship wars" have raged for a while in churches
and will probably do so as long as there are people with differing
opinions, ages, and preferences. Sometimes there are valid
points of reference, sometimes not. But, in every situation, there
are those who think a certain type of music is better suited for
worship and Christian expression.

Be a woman of hope by remembering that the energy of
the accompaniment or the coolness of the lyrics should never
outshine the message of doctrine or redemption. Pray for your
church's musical team.

* *

*Lord, guide those in music ministry at my church.
Give them inspiration and wisdom. Amen.*

121

TWO KINDS OF GROWTH

Yet more and more believers in the Lord joined them,
both men and women in really large numbers.
ACTS 5:14 PHILLIPS

A growing church, spiritually and numerically, is the hope and goal of every pastor and every sincere Christian. No serious follower of Christ wishes her church to remain small in number and immature in faith. Growth is usually a sign of health.

The early Church in the book of Acts experienced unusual and extraordinary growth. We will probably not replicate what happened in those unique days right after Pentecost. But we can be women of hope who contribute to our local church growth by doing our part—growing personally by reading and studying, and growing numerically by inviting and bringing others to church with us.

. . . .

Lord God, You give life and bring growth to Your
Church. Do that for mine. In Jesus' name. Amen.

ORGANIZED AND ORGANIC

*"And the master said to the servant, 'Go out to
the highways and hedges and compel people
to come in, that my house may be filled.' "*

LUKE 14:23 ESV

Churches do not grow by accident. And real church growth is not built on gimmicks or promotions. Measurable, healthful, biblical church growth happens from outreach.

Outreach may be an organized system within the church where teams of people go out into the community—in bus ministry, meet-and-greet community events, witnessing campaigns—and it may be organic in nature as individual believers in the congregation share Christ where they work and where they shop and where they play golf and drink coffee. Be a woman of hope by sharing your HOPE with those around you.

. . . .

*Heavenly Father, make me Your mouthpiece
today in a hurting world. Amen.*

COMMISSIONED FOR SERVICE

*While they were worshiping the Lord and fasting, the Holy
Spirit said, "Set apart for me Barnabas and Saul for the
work to which I have called them." Then after fasting and
praying they laid their hands on them and sent them off.*

ACTS 13:2–3 ESV

When a church has a heart for missions, it will have a heart
for people. The reason for sending missionaries is to bring
the Gospel to every person. Many times, there will be a
commissioning service with special prayers for those leaving.
You can do your part by praying for the ones who serve in far-
off places or maybe by going yourself if God wills.

* *

*You, O Lord, commission and ordain Your servants
to take the Gospel to the uttermost parts of the earth.
Thank You for loving all the people of the world. Amen.*

FELLOWSHIP AND FOOD

*And day after day they regularly assembled in the temple
with united purpose, and in their homes they broke bread
[including the Lord's Supper]. They partook of their food
with gladness and simplicity and generous hearts.*

ACTS 2:46 AMPC

Who doesn't love a church potluck?

Tables and tables of casseroles and mashed potatoes and
sweet corn and rolls followed by tables of pies and cakes and
gooey desserts of every sort. Ahh, the wonder of it!

It seems that the congregation of the early church had some
kind of shared meals too. Of course, they would have the Lord's
Supper, but also regular kinds of meals together. Right at the
beginning, they realized as the Spirit led them that fellowship
among believers is important.

* *

*Lord Jesus, You instituted the Lord's Supper
and You enjoyed fellowship with Your friends in
Bethany. We need to follow Your example. Amen.*

PLUG IN AND SERVE

The Twelve [apostles] convened the multitude of the disciples and said, It is not seemly or desirable or right that we should have to give up or neglect [preaching] the Word of God in order to attend to serving at tables and superintending the distribution of food.

ACTS 6:2 AMPC

There is a ministry for everyone in the local church. There are unseen jobs and public jobs. There are quiet positions and public positions. There are ministries suited to certain gifts.

Be a woman who brings hope to her church by asking to be plugged into a ministry or church organization that will match your abilities and that will allow you to contribute. If everyone did this, we would have more workers than we could ever use.

Dear Lord of the Church, keep us in Your grace. Help me to help my church. Amen.

HOPE FOR HEALTH

HEALTH CHOICES AND SELF-CONTROL

*In [exercising] knowledge [develop] self-control, and
in [exercising] self-control [develop] steadfastness
(patience, endurance), and in [exercising]
steadfastness [develop] godliness (piety).*

2 PETER 1:6 AMPC

Many of our health concerns in modern times are often affected by what we eat. Most of us are usually not able to control all the ingredients used or the substances added to our foods. We know it is more healthful to eat organically grown whole foods and that there are some elements that are problematic for certain people, such as sugar, gluten, dairy, dyes, etc.

But all of us can benefit from a careful approach to the table. It is difficult to change eating habits formed in childhood but, with God's help, we can make healthier choices even in small ways, which will result in better health.

*Lord, today help me to exercise self-control by choosing
what is best for my body in every way I can. Amen.*

KNOWN IN EVERY DETAIL

*We possess this precious treasure [the divine Light of
the Gospel] in [frail, human] vessels of earth, that the
grandeur and exceeding greatness of the power may
be shown to be from God and not from ourselves.*

2 CORINTHIANS 4:7 AMPC

Much as it distresses us at times to acknowledge it, our bodies
are subject to the principle of death at work in our fallen world.
They wear out and become diseased and fail to work in the
ways they should.

The way to be a woman of hope about health is to anchor
our serenity in the God who is aware of every detail of our lives,
including every hair of our heads and every cell in our bodies.
Nothing will pass by His care of us.

* *

*Holy Father, thank You for knowing everything
about me. I put my health in Your hands. Amen.*

TRUST IN THE MAKER

"Are not two sparrows sold for a penny? And not one of them will fall to the ground apart from your Father. . . . Fear not, therefore; you are of more value than many sparrows."

MATTHEW 10:29, 31 ESV

It's a good thing to have a medical team in which you have confidence. Whether we are young women approaching marriage or women in our childbearing years, women undergoing midlife changes or women experiencing failing health in our sunset years, most of us will need to visit a doctor at some point.

But the most important trust to have is in God, who watches over us. He made our female bodies, and He knows exactly how they work and all the complications that can arise. Be a woman of hope by trusting Him in all the unknowns.

. . . .

Lord, I bring to You my specific health needs today. In Jesus' name. Amen.

DUST LIKE US

"For you are dust, and to dust you shall return."
GENESIS 3:19 ESV

*As a father shows compassion to his children, so the
LORD shows compassion to those who fear him. For he
knows our frame; he remembers that we are dust.*
PSALM 103:13–14 ESV

When a baby is born, she begins to die. That is not a very
affirming thought as we gaze into our newborn's fresh little
face, but it is true, nonetheless. Since sin entered the world and
the curse of death passed onto all of us, we begin to deteriorate
as soon as we emerge from the womb. We are made of dust.

Jesus became incarnate in flesh so that He could share the
experience of being dust. And because of His sacrificial death
for us, someday we will no longer be dust but glorified like Him.

* *

*Creator God, thank You for Your compassion and for
sending Jesus to experience life and death for me. Amen.*

HE UNDERSTANDS OUR DISORDERS

There was a woman who had had a discharge of blood for
twelve years, and though she had spent all her living on
physicians, she could not be healed by anyone. She came
up behind him and touched the fringe of his garment,
and immediately her discharge of blood ceased.
LUKE 8:43–44 ESV

God instituted hygiene laws for His people in the Old Testament
to keep them healthy in primitive conditions and to illustrate
concepts about His character. The woman in this well-known
Bible story had a disorder that made her perpetually unclean.
She was isolated socially; she was restricted from the church,
probably anemic, and lonely.

God understands our sensitive and delicate conditions. We
can bring them to Him.

* *

Heavenly Father, I cannot touch Jesus' robe as this
woman did, but I bring to You my need today. Amen.

MASTER OF WINDS AND VIRUSES

He arose and left the synagogue and entered Simon's
house. Now Simon's mother-in-law was ill with a high
fever, and they appealed to him on her behalf. And he
stood over her and rebuked the fever, and it left her,
and immediately she rose and began to serve them.

LUKE 4:38–39 ESV

All of us have had a situation arise of a close relative getting unusually sick or having a serious health need, whether caused by an unexpected injury or from a genetic disorder. When that happens, we know the comfort we feel when others tell us "I'll be praying about that."

Jesus came to Simon Peter's house and rebuked the fever making his mother-in-law ill. Just as He talked to violent winds in nature, He spoke to viruses in nature. And both obeyed. He is Master of all.

. . . .

Lord Jesus, I am so glad that You are the Master of
the Universe and all nature must obey You. Amen.

HEALTH STEWARDS

*Miriam and Aaron spoke against Moses because of the
Cushite woman whom he had married, for he had married
a Cushite woman. . . . And the anger of the LORD was kindled
against them, and he departed. When the cloud removed from
over the tent, behold, Miriam was leprous, like snow. . . . And
Moses cried to the LORD, "O God, please heal her—please."*
NUMBERS 12:1, 9–10, 13 ESV

It is wrong for us to assume that every illness is a result of sin
on the part of the sufferer. However, there are times when that
is actually the case. If we go against what we know to do for
our bodies, we are actually sinning against them. And there
are consequences.

Moses pleaded for her healing, and God had mercy. In our
situations, sometimes He may heal and sometimes not. We
must take heed to our decisions so that we may enjoy as good
of health, if possible.

. . . .

*Lord, You are the God who expects us to take
care of ourselves. Give me wisdom. Amen.*

133

EVERY HEALING MOMENT

*There was in Joppa a disciple named Tabitha, which,
translated, means Dorcas. She was full of good works
and acts of charity. In those days she became ill and died,
and when they had washed her, they laid her in an upper
room. . . . But Peter put them all outside, and knelt down and
prayed; and turning to the body he said, "Tabitha, arise."
And she opened her eyes, and when she saw Peter she sat
up. And he gave her his hand and raised her up. Then,
calling the saints and widows, he presented her alive.*
ACTS 9:36–37, 40–41 ESV

God is the ultimate Healer. Many times, He uses doctors and
scientists. It is unlikely that we will ever witness a raising
from the dead, but we must not hesitate to bring to Him all our
occasions for healing and let Him work as He will.

- -

*God of Heaven, You hold in Your hands every moment of
healing and miracle. Today, I bring my health to You. Amen.*

HOLY AND SEPARATED

*Whatever parts the hoof and is cloven-footed and
chews the cud, among the animals, you may
eat. Nevertheless, among those that chew the
cud or part the hoof, you shall not eat these.*
LEVITICUS 11:3–4 ESV

Most of us are thankful that we are not required to keep the ceremonial laws of the Old Testament. But besides helping His people to stay healthy in primitive conditions, God instituted dietary laws to help them understand and to illustrate for them the idea of separation of the clean and unclean, the concept of holiness.

Yet, we would still do well to remember that the animals that were considered unclean in the Old Testament are generally not as healthful as others. Limiting our consumption of certain types of meat might have unexpected health benefits for us too!

· ·

*Father God, You are holy in all You are and
do. Purify me too, from the inside out. Amen.*

NEVER FORGOTTEN

"Shall not the Judge of all the earth do what is just?"
GENESIS 18:25 ESV

There are times in our health journey when we feel that we are not seen and that God has forgotten us. Our enemy, Satan, wants to get us to believe in those moments that we are not important to the Father, that He is too busy with other things and other people to notice our pain, our anguish, our life-altering circumstances.

But the Father, the Judge of all the earth, the Holy One, cannot and will not forget those who trust in Him. And He will do what is right in our lives. We cannot go by our understanding or by how things appear. We must trust His sovereign will and His holy character. He is trustworthy.

. . . .

Lord, I trust You today more than my own
understanding. I choose to believe in You. Amen.

HOPE FOR COMMUNITY

SAFETY COMES FROM THE LORD

*In peace I will both lie down and sleep; for you
alone, O LORD, make me dwell in safety.*

PSALM 4:8 ESV

Safety in our communities is a precious commodity.

The psalmist David knew what it was to lay down to sleep in volatile situations—on the run from King Saul who was trying to kill him, in the palace of a pagan King, in hiding from one of his sons who was staging a coup in the kingdom. And no doubt, David had spent a few nights in the fields with his sheep. But in all these situations, safety comes from the Lord.

And so it is with us. Let's do whatever we can to bring the hope of the Lord to our communities.

. . . .

*Father in heaven, I ask You to guide me as I
try to bring Your hope to my community. Amen.*

PRAYING FOR YOUR STREET

Whoever pursues righteousness and kindness
will find life, righteousness, and honor.
PROVERBS 21:21 ESV

Morality in our communities goes beyond meetings by the town council or homeowners association; morality is also determined by what happens in the homes along the streets.

On almost every street in every community in every town across the nation, there is immorality. Sexual sin has slithered into our neighborhoods and destroyed our marriages and families and even our understanding of gender and the value of life. Being a woman of hope in your community means praying for the homes along your street and asking God to bring the light of righteousness.

. . . .

Holy God, I pray that You would put a desire in my neighbors'
hearts to pursue righteous lives. In Jesus' name. Amen.

THE FOUNDATION OF EDUCATION

The fear of the LORD is the beginning of wisdom;
all those who practice it have a good understanding.
PSALM 111:10 ESV

A predominant influence in our communities is our schools. Those who understand God's Word know that the faith and morality of scripture actually lay a perfect foundation for learning other subjects. When we have a solid belief in our purpose as created beings and a firm grasp on how we should treat others, we are ready to learn the other rudiments that society proposes. Pray for your local teachers' unions to return to godly principles.

. . . .

Dear Lord, please open the eyes of the educators
in my local school system. In Jesus' name. Amen.

WORK FROM THE CHURCH

I was glad when they said unto me,
Let us go into the house of the LORD.
PSALM 122:1 KJV

A community is only as good as the doctrine taught in its churches. The landscape of our country in years past was filled with God-honoring churches, and the nation showed the result.

You can bring hope to your community by praying for the churches you pass on your way to work or worship. If they are false churches, pray that God would open their eyes. If they are churches wandering in doctrine, pray that God would awaken them. If they are struggling churches, pray that God would invigorate them. God has chosen to work through local churches; pray that they are in a position to do that work.

• •

Dear God, work in the churches of my community; may the pastors honor Your Word in their lives and teaching. Amen.

STREETS AND NEIGHBORHOODS

*Thus says the Lord of hosts: Old men and old women
shall again sit in the streets of Jerusalem, each with staff
in hand because of great age. And the streets of the city
shall be full of boys and girls playing in its streets.*

ZECHARIAH 8:4–5 ESV

This scripture paints an image that all of us would like to see in our neighborhoods—a safe and happy place where families flourish and the elderly are revered and protected. The prophet wrote these words to the people of Judah who were in exile.

We do not have a similar promise for our present neighborhoods, but we can claim the words of the Bible when it promises blessing to those who honor God. We can be women who pray for the families we pass as we walk in the evening.

• •

*Father in heaven, use me to intercede for
my street and my neighborhood. Amen.*

ALIGNING COMMUNITY VALUES

"You shall stand up before the gray head and honor the face
of an old man, and you shall fear your God: I am the LORD."
LEVITICUS 19:32 ESV

Homes for the elderly and sick exist in most communities and towns. Some of them are called assisted-living centers, some are referred to as long-term care facilities, others are called nursing homes, but they are usually filled with residents struggling with either aging or progressive, debilitating conditions.

Our society has traditionally respected those who are aging, and that is a direct biblical principle. When we show honor to those who are older, we are aligning our values with God's. Be a woman of hope for your community by praying for the care facilities and for the people in them.

- -

Dear Lord, let my community show honor to those
who are elderly and let me lead the way. Amen.

SPECIAL NEEDS AMONG US

*As he passed by, he saw a man blind from birth. And his
disciples asked him, "Rabbi, who sinned, this man or
his parents, that he was born blind?" Jesus answered,
"It was not that this man sinned, or his parents, but
that the works of God might be displayed in him."*
JOHN 9:1–3 ESV

Every community has these special needs among its members.
We know from the words of Jesus in the scripture above
that the presence of special needs is not necessarily a result of
sin, though there are times when irresponsible actions on the
part of the parents can cause such problems. But we do know
that He expects us to do our part to care about them.

. . . .

*God, bless those in my community who offer
help to those with special needs and keep
these dear people safe and cared for. Amen.*

CARE FOR THE NEEDY

*"For I was hungry and you gave me food, I was thirsty and
you gave me drink, I was a stranger and you welcomed
me, I was naked and you clothed me, I was sick and
you visited me, I was in prison and you came to me."*
MATTHEW 25:35–36 ESV

With our advanced medical knowledge, life expectancy is longer
than it was a century or so ago. And that means that many will
become caregivers to their aging parents or other relatives.

Jesus told His listeners that whenever we provide care
for someone who is needy we are actually doing a service to
Him. We have not usually thought of this verse in reference to
caregivers, but it does seem to apply. Pray for the caregivers
in your community; they need it.

. . . .

*Dear Lord, bless those in my community who are
sitting with a loved one today. In Jesus' name. Amen.*

RESPONDING TO NEARBY NEEDS

*Better is a neighbor who is near
than a brother who is far away.*
PROVERBS 27:10 ESV

First responders see things that few of the rest of the community see. They respond to alarms and tragedies while the rest of us relax at home and wonder where the siren is going. They deal with the aftermath of horrific images and the guilt of not being able to save some of the victims they were called to rescue. They are our neighbors "who are near." They can help us in ways that even our own families cannot.

The first responders in your community need your prayers and support. Thank God for their willingness to serve and for the skills they possess.

. . . .

*Father God, bless the first responders in my community.
Today, may they have healing in their minds and
rest in their bodies. In Jesus' name. Amen.*

LOCAL LAYERS MATTER

Every Christian ought to obey the civil authorities,
for all legitimate authority is derived from God's
authority, and the existing authority is appointed
under God. To oppose authority then is to oppose God,
and such opposition is bound to be punished.

ROMANS 13:1–2 PHILLIPS

Government is important, down to the local level. Those who comprise the governing body in your town—mayor, city council, school board—are the first layer of rule to which the Bible tells us to give honor. Authority is ordained by God and is instituted on earth for our good and protection.

When we begin to disregard any layer of authority, we call into question the whole idea of structure and submission and the hierarchy of rule. Of course, God doesn't bless tyranny, but He does institute basic civil authority.

* *

Lord, give my local authorities the wisdom to lead
my community and the courage to do it well. Amen.

HOPE FOR EMOTIONS
HELP FOR THE DISQUIET

*Why are you cast down, O my inner self? And why should
you moan over me and be disquieted within me? Hope in
God and wait expectantly for Him, for I shall yet praise
Him, Who is the help of my countenance, and my God.*

PSALM 42:11 AMPC

Anxiety disorders have been around since ancient times. In
the Bible, we find that many of the emotions we face have been
addressed by the inspired writers.

Anxiety causes a disquiet in the inner self. It makes the
thoughts swirl and the brain seem noisy with confusion. It is
difficult to focus and challenging to believe what others say.

The psalmist points to the Lord as the Help for which we
can wait expectantly. He is trustworthy.

* *

*Heavenly Father, I look to You for the calm
I cannot bring to myself. I wait on You. Amen.*

GET RID OF PRIDE

God sets Himself against the proud (the insolent, the
overbearing, the disdainful, the presumptuous, the
boastful)—[and He opposes, frustrates, and defeats
them], but gives grace (favor, blessing) to the humble.

1 PETER 5:5 AMPC

Pride is an ugly sin. It was the sin of Lucifer, the brightest angel of heaven, who fell and became the archenemy of the God who created him. It was the sin of Eve who lusted for more than God had given, thinking she deserved more and instead lost what she did have when she sinned.

Pride causes us to do ugly things and feel ugly ways. God hates pride. But He gives grace to those who are humble. If you struggle with feelings of pride, make a deliberate choice to humble yourself and ask for God's help to surrender it.

. . . .

Father God, reveal to me any pride in my heart
and give me the grace to deal with it. Amen.

AN ONGOING SURRENDER

Exercise foresight and be on the watch. . .in order that
no root of resentment (rancor, bitterness, or hatred)
shoots forth and causes trouble and bitter torment, and
the many become contaminated and defiled by it.

The aftermath of betrayal is a wash of terrible emotion. Whether the deed is done by a husband or friend or family member, the knowledge that a person you trusted would sell you out is almost too much to take. After the initial shock and hurt comes anger and then resentment and then bitterness.

The way to stop the progression is to put the pain in the Father's hands continually, over and over again. Some hurts take a process of redemption and healing. This is one of them. Lean on Him minute by minute.

* *

Lord God, I cannot process this properly on my own. Please
help me with these feelings of betrayal. In Jesus' name. Amen.

DEPRESSION IS A QUIET THIEF

*I am weary with my groaning; all night I soak my pillow with
tears, I drench my couch with my weeping. My eye grows dim
because of grief; it grows old because of all my enemies.*

PSALM 6:6–7 AMPC

Depression is a quiet oppressor. It steals the joy from everyday
living and smothers the life out of anticipation. It takes the
breath out of life and robs memories of their sparkle. It can
be a serious, clinical type of disturbance or a minor one with
a hormonal, chemical, or contextual cause. But for every heart
crying into a pillow tonight, our God cares.

There is hope for the emotion of depression because all
earthly feelings are subject to His power.

* *

*Lord, lead me to the right resources for my depression
and heal me as You will. In Jesus' name. Amen.*

SIGNIFICANCE AND STARS

He determines and counts the number of
the stars; He calls them all by their names.
PSALM 147:4 AMPC

Feelings of insignificance plague the human family. We are tempted to think we are only a number, a face, another link in the infinite chain of history.

There is a company that advertises the fact that they will name a star after your friend or relative and send them a certificate for a special occasion. While we understand why someone would think that's a good idea, it is a little humorous when one considers that they have already been named by God.

And the God who names planets and heavenly bodies comprised of burning gases knows your name too. You are significant and known. That should give you hope.

. . . .

Dear God, You count the stars and know where they
go; You see me right now too. Thank You. Amen.

VICTORY IN THE MIND

Wrath is cruel and anger is an overwhelming
flood, but who is able to stand before jealousy?
PROVERBS 27:4 AMPC

Feelings of jealousy or envy can come upon us like a tidal wave. In response to events taking place or the words of someone else, suddenly we feel the wave of negative and even sinful emotion rushing toward us. In that moment, we must make a choice to honor Christ both in our outward response and in the attitude we allow to remain. No one can force us to harbor feelings of jealousy or to act in un-Christlike ways.

Satan's favorite battleground on which to engage us is the mind. We need the power of the Holy Spirit and the sword of the Word in order to defeat Him.

. . . .

I surrender, O Lord, my emotions to You before
the moment even comes. Help me maintain
that surrender in the crisis. Amen.

FOLLOWING THE PATTERN

O LORD, my heart is not lifted up; my eyes
are not raised too high; I do not occupy myself
with things too great and too marvelous for me.
PSALM 131:1 ESV

Arrogance usually feels repulsive to those looking on. When someone appears to think too highly of themselves and to elevate their accomplishments and opinions over others, it does not draw friends. There are times when we misjudge someone who is quiet or shy and believe she is being aloof when she is not. It is important to give everyone the benefit of the doubt.

Humility, a teachable spirit, and a ready smile will go a long way in helping us be approachable by others. When we are tempted to foster the emotion of arrogance, we must remind ourselves that, as Christ followers, He is our pattern in all things.

* *

Holy God, nothing I can do or think or say can come close
to Your glory; let me stay humble as Your servant. Amen.

MEET ANGER AT THE DOOR

If you are angry, be sure that it is not out of
wounded pride or bad temper. Never go to bed
angry—don't give the devil that sort of foothold.
EPHESIANS 4:26 PHILLIPS

Anger is a normal human emotion in response to an injustice, real or perceived. There are appropriate times to be angry—when an innocent person is mistreated or when someone in authority is abusive or when God's laws are being mocked by evildoers.

But there are also inappropriate angry responses that are predicated on our own selfish wishes or perceived rights. When we are angry because someone didn't fulfill our expectations or made us look bad or caused us inconvenience, we must be careful to sort out our motivation for response and choose to follow what the Spirit is saying.

Feelings of anger must be met at the door by truth and temperance.

* *

Lord Jesus, You had so many reasons to be angry
while You were on earth, but You never expressed it in
unholy ways. Help me to follow Your example. Amen.

HATERS IN HEART

Everyone who hates his brother is a murderer, and you
know that no murderer has eternal life abiding in him.
1 JOHN 3:15 ESV

The word *hate* is used a lot and often in ways that do not truly reflect the strong meaning of the word. We can hate anything from soggy bread to traffic jams. Often, when we use the word, we really mean that we are irritated by something.

But the animosity and malice of real hatred for another person is strongly condemned by the Bible. There is no way that any of us can harbor hatred for someone and still follow Christ. Hating makes a murderer in spirit.

We can be women of hope by surrendering our strong emotions to God and allowing His transforming power to be revealed in us.

. . . .

God, You are perfectly loving, even toward those who curse
You. Give me power not to hate anyone. In Jesus' name. Amen.

WHEN NOT *IF*

When I am afraid, I put my trust in you. In God, whose
word I praise, in God I trust; I shall not be afraid.
PSALM 56:3–4 ESV

It is interesting that the wording of this verse is "when" and
not "if." It seems that the Bible acknowledges that there will
be moments when the uncertainties of this earthly life will
cause the emotion of fear to rise up inside us. But what we do
with our fear is what matters. When we feel the rise of fear,
we must meet it with an equal measure of trust. This is not a
trust that nothing bad will ever happen but a trust that, when
it does, we will not be alone, a trust that says He is in charge
and nothing is random.

* *

O God, there is no one more trustworthy than
You. I place my life in Your hands. Amen.

HOPE FOR REST
LONGING FOR SLEEP

*It is in vain that you rise up early and go late to rest, eating
the bread of anxious toil; for he gives to his beloved sleep.*
PSALM 127:2 ESV

Are you a light or heavy sleeper? If you're married, your
husband is probably the opposite. It seems to work that way,
in the same manner that chilly people marry people with
overheated internal thermostats and spenders marry savers
and fast drivers marry slowpokes. It just happens that way.
Or God allows it that way.

But regardless of your husband's sleep habits, you need
hope for your own rest. Are you nursing a fussy baby? Sitting
up with a sick child? Suffering with midlife insomnia?

God gives us rest at night, but sometimes our world doesn't
cooperate. Just remember that these are but seasons and the
God who put the moon out tonight will hang it there again
tomorrow.

. . . .

*Thank You, O Lord, for making
the night and giving us rest. Amen.*

157

DO YOUR PART

*"Six days work shall be done, but on the seventh day you
shall have a Sabbath of solemn rest, holy to the Lord.
Whoever does any work on it shall be put to death."*

EXODUS 35:2 ESV

God made the universe and everything in it in just six days. On
the seventh day He rested and sanctified it as holy.

By doing this, not only did He create a pattern for us of work
and rest, but He signified that rest is actually very important—it
is sacred.

Some of us are better at resting than others. Some of us
have trouble kicking off our shoes and sitting on the couch
doing nothing, reading nothing, thinking nothing. But it doesn't
matter what our natural inclination is because God tells us to
obey as an act of the will, not feeling.

• •

*Creator God, thank You for setting the example of
rest for us. I want to value Your sacred day. Amen.*

REST AND ENJOY

There is nothing better for a man than that he should eat
and drink and make himself enjoy good in his labor.
Even this, I have seen, is from the hand of God.
ECCLESIASTES 2:24 AMPC

Because our lives usually run on the scale of global proportions, we forget to find enjoyment in the ordinary. But when we do, that's a kind of rest.

Through the means of technology, we are exposed to the high highs and low lows of people from all over the world. Our own little bits of happiness in our homes and gardens and favorite easy chair can seem paltry in comparison. But the wise man was inspired to remind us that these simple pleasures are the gift of God. And when we enjoy them, we enter into a type of rest that is good and blessed.

* *

Thank You, O God, for creating simple pleasures.
I will enjoy them with a full heart. Amen.

THE REST OF EATING

Go, eat your bread with joy, and drink
your wine with a merry heart.
ECCLESIASTES 9:7 ESV

Do you bolt your food?

Our grandmothers used to use this phrase to refer to the action of wolfing down the contents of one's plate without enjoying conversation or giving the stomach the proper time to process. It was thought to be unhealthy for the digestive system (and it probably is).

But one reason to enjoy mealtime as a kind of rest is because it is another way to say "thanks" to the God who provided it. Few of us would enjoy giving a gift to a child or grandchild only to see them tear the wrapping from it, caress it quickly, smile, put it down, and jump up to do chores. Entering into this kind of pleasure is restful, and our Father above calls us to it.

. . . .

Lord, thank You for mealtimes and the provisions
from You. I will do my best to enjoy them. Amen.

CADENCE AND GRATITUDE

"You shall come to your grave in ripe old age,
like a sheaf gathered up in its season."
JOB 5:26 ESV

There is a kind of death that, though sad and unwelcome as the curse always is, reminds us that God finishes what He begins, and a life well lived has a fitting ending. These are the types of graves that are graced with a tombstone that captions a life that was lived long and righteous, full of adventure and promise, influencing others to do good things and ending in a dignified, quiet manner. This is the type of death we would all prefer but only some are granted. But they remind us that, in God's hands, even the results of a curse can be redeemed and beautified.

. . . .

God of the Ages, thank You for providing the
cadence to the end of life as well as to the beginning.
I trust You with the details of mine. Amen.

REST AREAS FOR THE MIND

*But this I call to mind, and therefore I have hope:
the steadfast love of the LORD never ceases; his
mercies never come to an end; they are new
every morning; great is your faithfulness.*
LAMENTATIONS 3:21–23 ESV

Our minds are constantly on alert, fielding questions and bits of news, absorbing information, and processing the drama of everyday life. They need a break.

We can rest our minds by physical sleep. This rejuvenates the biological parts of the brain. And we can rest our minds in a spiritual sense by having hope in the steadfast love of the Lord and in His mercies that are new every morning. He is faithful, and our minds can sigh and lean into that for as long as they need.

* *

*Father in heaven, I praise You for Your steadfast love
for me and for the spiritual rest I find in Your Word. Amen.*

RESTED AND READY

The LORD is my light and my salvation; whom shall I fear?
the LORD is the strength of my life; of whom shall I be afraid?
PSALM 27:1 KJV

The mind is a powerful entity, and it exerts tremendous sway over the whole body. If one believes she cannot do a thing, whether it be ice skating or baking a cake, her body will absorb her opinion and she probably won't.

God's Word reminds us that we have nothing to fear when He is the strength of our lives. Spiritual rest comes from putting absolute confidence in His ability to shore up our inability.

. . . .

God my Father, I am always amazed at the strength
I gain from being in Your presence. When I do,
my mind is rested and ready to take up the next
challenge. I gladly owe my rest to You. Amen.

THE REST OF OLD AGE

*The righteous flourish like the palm tree and grow like
a cedar in Lebanon. They are planted in the house of
the LORD; they flourish in the courts of our God. They
still bear fruit in old age; they are ever full of sap and
green, to declare that the LORD is upright; he is my
rock, and there is no unrighteousness in him.*

PSALM 92:12–15 ESV

Old women don't have babies. Old trees may totter and fall. Old
things don't work well. But old people who love God are as good
as ever in their spiritual selves. The scripture says they will still
bear fruit in old age. And they are full of sap—full of strength
and zest for living. That sounds like a rested old age to me.

. . . .

*Heavenly Father, let me rest in You so that when
I get old, I will still be full of vigor for You. Amen.*

VACATIONS FOR BODY AND MIND

The apostles returned to Jesus and reported to him every detail of what they had done and taught. "Now come along to some quiet place by yourselves, and rest for a little while," said Jesus, for there were people coming and going incessantly so that they had not even time for meals.

MARK 6:31 PHILLIPS

Vacations are the bright spots on our calendars. We look forward to them all year.

Jesus knew that His disciples needed a little while away from the work of ministry so that they could eat in peace and rest themselves, physically and spiritually. We need that too. Being a woman of hope, a woman of rest, means being realistic about appropriate self-care. A vacation should be on the list.

* *

Lord God, You know the rest I need. Help me plan a restful vacation this year. Amen.

RESTING IN ETERNAL EMBRACE

*Then I heard a voice from Heaven, saying, "Write this!
From henceforth happy are the dead who die in the
Lord!" "Happy indeed," says the Spirit, "for they rest
from their labours and their deeds go with them!"*
REVELATION 14:13 PHILLIPS

The Bible is clear that when we are absent from our earthly
bodies, we are in God's eternal presence. The liturgy for a
graveside ceremony may reference the fact that the body is
resting until the final resurrection. And while the dust of the
body lies in the ground, the spirit of the believer is resting in
the eternal embrace of the One who made her and died for her.
This is the truest kind of rest there can be.

* *

*Heavenly Lord, I want to rest in You for eternity and
share Your heaven. Thank You for making that
possible through Jesus. In His name. Amen.*

HOPE FOR A LEGACY

A LASTING IMPRINT

*He makes the barren woman to be a homemaker and a joyful
mother of [spiritual] children. Praise the Lord! (Hallelujah!)*
PSALM 113:9 AMPC

Leaving a legacy is important, especially as a child of God.

We will leave a legacy whether we try to or not. The log of
our actions, words, decisions, and interactions will be recorded
in the memories of those who knew us. How wonderful if
that log is defined by a heart for God and a commitment to
His ways.

One of the ways a Christian woman leaves a legacy is
through the spiritual children she nurtures. Even if she is not
a biological mother, she may be a spiritual mother, leaving a
lasting imprint on the lives of those she nurtured in the faith.

. . . .

*God of all grace, let Your love so fill me that I may be
a spiritual mother to many who come after me. Amen.*

WHAT COUNTS

And he shall be like a tree firmly planted [and tended]
by the streams of water, ready to bring forth its fruit
in its season; its leaf also shall not fade or wither; and
everything he does shall prosper [and come to maturity].
Not so the wicked [those disobedient and living without
God are not so]. But they are like the chaff [worthless,
dead, without substance] which the wind drives away.

PSALM 1:3–4 AMPC

There is no significance to chaff—it is refuse, litter, worthless.
Both in the wheat field and in a life, whatever is chaff does not
add anything of note. Too many women are living their lives in
"chaffy" ways and building for themselves a life of no lasting
significance.

The way to have a significant legacy is to be like a tree
planted in God, and then everything we do for Him will prosper.

. . . .

Father in heaven, keep me today from worthless
living. I want my life to count. Amen.

PARTS OF SPEECH

Let the words of my mouth, and the meditation
of my heart, be acceptable in thy sight,
O Lord, my strength, and my redeemer.
PSALM 19:14 KJV

There is hope for your legacy when you guard the words of your mouth and the meditations of your mind. Careless speech, sown to the wind, does not profit anyone and certainly does not stand the test of time. But words that are passed through the oversight of the Holy Spirit will have lasting effect and will grace the memory of those who knew you.

Legacy words are thoughtful and purposeful, sometimes strong, sometimes quiet, but always with the purpose of instructing others in the way of righteousness. These words will live on when we do not.

. . . .

Lord in heaven, You created speech with all its expressions
and modifiers and participles and prepositions and nuances.
Today, let me use my language to leave a legacy. Amen.

A STORY TO TELL

Give her of the fruit of her hands, and let her
own works praise her in the gates [of the city]!
PROVERBS 31:31 AMPC

All of us are good at something, and when we go to be with Jesus someday, those we leave will look through our things and remember what we did. The possessions we have will tell a story about us.

A woman who wants to leave a legacy of hope will use her talents in ways that glorify the God who gave them and that bless others around her. And someday when they stand around her casket, they'll have more to say than "Doesn't she look good!"

. . . .

Dear Lord, live Your life through my abilities
and let me use them to honor You. Amen.

A FRAGRANT LIFE

Thanks be to God who leads us, wherever we are, on his own triumphant way and makes our knowledge of him spread throughout the world like a lovely perfume!

2 CORINTHIANS 2:14 PHILLIPS

One of the things you will notice about a woman's closet is that her clothing may bear her scent. After a loved one dies, the family may draw comfort from inhaling the fragrance left on things she wore. The scent reminds them of the loveliness of that life.

In a similar way, the lives we live as believers leave a scent behind us. The attitudes and actions we had remain in the memories of those who knew us and remind them of us. Of course, all of us are human and therefore have moments of deep humanity. But the overall tone of our lives can bear a sweet fragrance that ever leaves a legacy of grace.

. . . .

Dear Jesus, I want my life to have the fragrance of love and service like Yours. Amen.

THE HEART OF HOME

Her children rise up and call her blessed;
her husband also, and he praises her.
PROVERBS 31:28 ESV

While it isn't lauded as much today, homemaking is still biblically associated with Mom. One woman's husband told her that while he was the head of their home, she was its heart. That seems a lovely and accurate description of what God intended when He created the human family.

As women who are finding hope for the legacy we leave, we need to remind ourselves that the home we manage is very much a gift to our families and an important piece of how we will be remembered. Does this mean that spotless floors matter more than anything else? No. But it does mean that the way our home "feels" and "welcomes" its family is something our children will always remember.

· ·

Dear God, being a homemaker is a big
job. I need Your help and wisdom. Amen.

AN ANGEL GIFT AND A LEGACY

*To the woman he said, "I will surely multiply your pain
in childbearing; in pain you shall bring forth children."*
GENESIS 3:16 ESV

It has been said that grandchildren are God's reward for not killing your own kids!

Maybe there is something to the fact that grandchildren are rather a gift that appears. When our own children were carried and born, we were right there doing the work. And the Word of God is true—there was pain and suffering and inconvenience. But grandchildren are akin to an angel gift from heaven, borne by another yet remarkably like us. We can't help but be mesmerized by them. Still, if we want to leave a legacy to them, we will honor good guidelines for behavior in our homes still so that someday their true young forms will make us proud as they carry on our legacy.

· ·

*Dear God, thank You for grandchildren.
Help me leave a good legacy to mine. Amen.*

A TREASURE CHEST

Thy word is a lamp unto my feet, and a light unto my path.
PSALM 119:105 KJV

Families who are privileged to have a mother or grandmother who reads and writes in her Bible will discover a great treasure chest of wisdom—first, because it is God's Word and second, because it will have the flavor of her notes and the scrawl of her handwriting.

How we use our Bibles is important to our spiritual lives and to our legacy. Online Bibles deny us the thrill of actual handwriting on the pages, but they may still contain notes that we can treasure. If you are a Bible-believing and Bible-practicing Christian, then you have hope for your legacy. And others will delight in it.

* *

*Father God, thank You for Your Word that is
living and powerful. I love to read it. Amen.*

CONTENTS OF A LIFE

I only say this, let the builder be careful how he builds! The foundation is laid already, and no one can lay another, for it is Jesus Christ himself. But any man who builds on the foundation using as his material gold, silver, precious stones, wood, hay or stubble, must know that each man's work will one day be shown for what it is. The day will show it plainly enough, for the day will arise in a blaze of fire, and that fire will prove the nature of each man's work.
1 CORINTHIANS 3:11–13 PHILLIPS

Going through the belongings of someone who has died is both a pitiful and an enlightening activity. The common elements of human life are there—nail clippers, safety pins, coins, writing pens, etc. But someday, at the Judgment, the spiritual elements of our lives will be examined and tried by fire and only what is valuable will remain.

- -

O Judge of all the earth, show me what to value so that my life work will not be consumed as refuse. Amen.

CAPTION THAT TOMBSTONE

"Many women have done excellently,
but you surpass them all."
PROVERBS 31:29 ESV

What do you want on your tombstone?

Tombstones can tell us a lot about the people under them. Were they pompous or unassuming, wealthy or poor, Christian or not? Not always can we discern these things but oftentimes there are clues.

The words of the Proverbs writer would certainly be a compliment to any woman receiving them on her tombstone. But, of course, she would be gone when others read them. The important thing is to live now in such a way that these statements might honestly be said when we can no longer speak for ourselves.

* *

You will guide me in life, O God, and You will be
there when only my legacy remains. I praise
You for Your guiding hand in my life. Amen.

HOPE FOR ETERNITY
IT'S ON RECORD

*"They have conquered him by the blood of
the Lamb and by the word of their testimony,
for they loved not their lives even unto death."*

REVELATION 12:11 ESV

Testimony is a word closely tied to *testament*, which can signify the part of a person's will having to do with personal property. Even further, a testimony is evidence of something that happened and can have legal import. When we give a testimony in church, we are putting on the public record what has happened to us as the result of Christ's work in our lives.

The joy of heaven will be sharing our testimony and hearing those of others. By recounting the power of His blood and redemption that changed us and the trials through which He brought us, we will be part of the eternal record giving praise forever to the Lamb of God.

. . . .

*Jesus, Your death on the cross purchased my pardon and
gave me a testimony to share. I praise Your name. Amen.*

FINAL JOY

In whom we have redemption through his blood, the forgiveness of sins, according to the riches of his grace.
EPHESIANS 1:7 KJV

The word *redemption* means to buy back. That's what God did through Jesus—He was buying us back from the dominion, the slavery, of sin. He was restoring the original relationship mankind had with Him in the perfection of Eden. He was giving us the hope of being in His eternal presence someday.

The woman who has hope for eternity knows that her redemption is only because of Christ. And she does not lose sight of that in all the other messages around her. She holds fast to the riches of His grace and looks ahead to that perfect day.

* *

Dear God, thank You for buying me back from destruction. Use me to tell others about this hope. In Jesus' name. Amen.

HOPE FOR A REUNION

*The Lord himself will descend from heaven with a cry
of command, with the voice of an archangel, and with
the sound of the trumpet of God. And the dead in Christ
will rise first. Then we who are alive, who are left, will be
caught up together with them in the clouds to meet the
Lord in the air, and so we will always be with the Lord.
Therefore encourage one another with these words.*

1 THESSALONIANS 4:16–18 ESV

Much of the joy of eternity will be our reunion with those who have died before us—our family members, friends, Christian mentors, and acquaintances. And there will even be a sense of belonging with those whom we've never known on earth but who love the same Lord and inhabit the same heaven. We will forever be in glad reunion.

*Heavenly Father, I look forward to
spending eternity with those I love. Amen.*

HOPE BECAUSE OF A FATHER

But as it is, they desire a better country, that is, a heavenly one. Therefore God is not ashamed to be called their God, for he has prepared for them a city.
HEBREWS 11:16 ESV

Not every person on earth has a good father. While every living human has a biological father, a male who contributed to the genetic formation of a new being, not every human has the privilege of knowing that person in a fatherly role. And many times, it would be a horrific experience if it were even possible.

But God, our heavenly Father, will replace all the old bad ideas about fathers and fill them with Himself. For all eternity, we will be with Him and enjoy the good things He has prepared for us.

* *

Father in heaven, I look forward to sharing Your home someday. I love You. Amen.

HOPE FOR A HOME

"Let not your heart be troubled; you believe in God,
believe also in Me. In My Father's house are many
mansions; if it were not so, I would have told you. I
go to prepare a place for you. And if I go and prepare
a place for you, I will come again and receive you to
Myself; that where I am, there you may be also."

JOHN 14:1–3 NKJV

Some Bible translations say "rooms" or "dwelling places" while
others say "mansions."

Whatever they are, they will be perfect, perfectly suited for
us individually, perfectly constructed by the One who loves us.

In ancient Israel, the bridegroom built a new dwelling onto
his father's house before he went to marry his bride. In this
ancient visual, we understand more about our future with Christ.

. . . .

Lord Jesus, thank You for preparing a
place for me in heaven with You. Amen.

HOPE FOR A REWARD

Behold, I come quickly; and my reward is with me,
to give every man according as his work shall be.
REVELATION 22:12 KJV

If we love God, we keep His commandments. We don't do it for the reward; we do it for love. But, just as children look forward to awards after a competition, so we may look forward to the rewards God will give us as we finish our earthly race and step into His kingdom.

Jesus and the Gospel writers both mention rewards for what is done on earth. It is clear that God wants us to understand that He rewards faithfulness and diligence and along with those gleaming presentations will be His words, "Well done, good and faithful servant."

. . . .

Dear God, help me to be faithful on earth so that I
may hear Your wonderful words someday. Amen.

HOPE FOR THE RECKONING

*For we must all appear before the judgment seat of
Christ, so that each one may receive what is due for
what he has done in the body, whether good or evil.*

2 CORINTHIANS 5:10 ESV

Just like the yearly audit in the office or the annual inventory at
the business, there will be a great day of reckoning in eternity. The
books of records will be opened, and our lives will be examined.
On that great day, our ancestry won't matter; our educational
pedigree won't signify; our illustrious titles and accomplishments
won't tip the scale. What will matter is if we lived our redeemed
lives in ways that honored Christ and His Word.

Today, be a woman with hope for that day. Put God first in
every choice you make.

. . . .

*God, I want my earthly actions to reflect Christ on
that day of reckoning. Show me any lack. Amen.*

HOPE FOR A KING

On his robe and on his thigh he has a name
written, King of kings and Lord of lords.
REVELATION 19:16 ESV

Those who have lived in a country with royalty may have a better idea of what it will be to first see King Jesus. They are accustomed to the awe and splendor, to the automatic response to the ruling monarch. But regardless of our earthly country, we will, as one, fall on our faces before the One who will someday ride a white horse and be proclaimed King of kings.

Kings have the power to protect their subjects. Jesus will engage in battle with Satan, and He will win the victory. When Satan is bound, we will rejoice and enjoy forever in His kingdom.

. . . .

Lord Jesus, I look forward to bowing in Your presence
and living in Your kingdom for eternity. Amen.

HOPE FOR A REPLACEMENT

*"We who are still alive shall suddenly be utterly changed.
For this perishable nature of ours must be wrapped in
imperishability, these bodies which are mortal must be
wrapped in immortality. So when the perishable is lost in
the imperishable, the mortal lost in the immortal, this saying
will come true: 'Death is swallowed up in victory' 'O death,
where is your sting? O Hades, where is your victory?'"*

1 CORINTHIANS 15:52–54 PHILLIPS

The old department store Sears used to have a guarantee on
one brand of little boys' pants—if they wore out in the knees,
you could bring them in for a replacement. That's a little like
what will happen with us. We will exchange our old worn-out
bodies for replacements—new bodies like His resurrected
body. What a day that will be!

• •

*Thank You, Lord, for the promise of
a new body to have for eternity! Amen.*

HOPE FOR A CROWN

*Henceforth there is laid up for me the crown of
righteousness, which the Lord, the righteous judge,
will award to me on that day, and not only to me
but also to all who have loved his appearing.*

2 TIMOTHY 4:8 ESV

Most of us will never wear a crown on earth, except maybe a fake
tiara on our wedding day. But if we love Jesus and live our lives
for Him, we will someday have a real crown. How will it look?
How heavy will it be? Will God Himself actually hand them out?

We don't know the answers. But we do know that we will
probably offer them back to Jesus, the One who died for us.

Runners in the Olympic-type games of Paul's day were
crowned with a laurel wreath. But someday, Christ's followers
will be crowned with gold.

· ·

*Lord, help me to stay faithful and true so that
I will not lose my crown of glory with You. Amen.*

HOPE FOR A SONG

And they sang a new song, saying, "Worthy are you to take the scroll and to open its seals, for you were slain, and by your blood you ransomed people for God from every tribe and language and people and nation."
REVELATION 5:9 ESV

Music is a big part of earthly life, and it will be part of eternal life. God created music. It is one of His good gifts. And the Bible indicates that there will be singing and music in heaven and in the New Jerusalem. We will sing praises to Jesus, the Lamb of God. And that song will be beautiful beyond anything we currently know because it is the song that tells of our redemption from heaven's perspective.

· ·

Dear Lord, thank You for creating music both for this world and for the one to come. Amen.

HOPE FOR A NAME

"The one who conquers, I will make him a pillar in the temple of my God. Never shall he go out of it, and I will write on him the name of my God, and the name of the city of my God, the new Jerusalem, which comes down from my God out of heaven, and my own new name."

REVELATION 3:12 ESV

Our parents gave us our earthly names. They based it on many things—a loved relative, a high school friend, someone who died, the cool sound, a mother's surname, the popularity of the name, etc. We are identified by gender and family and many times, by ethnicity, according to our names.

Someday, we will receive God's name. And it will identify us as one of His, bought by the blood, redeemed, reconciled, and rewarded.

. . . .

Dear Lord, I look forward to receiving Your name someday in eternity. I love You. Amen.

HOPE FOR A STONE

"He who has an ear, let him hear what the Spirit says to the churches. To the one who conquers I will give some of the hidden manna, and I will give him a white stone, with a new name written on the stone that no one knows except the one who receives it."

REVELATION 2:17 ESV

We are told quite a bit about the jewels of heaven and the streets of gold and the gems used in the gates. But we are also told that there will be white stones with names on them, our new names, symbols of eternity with Him.

. . . .

Dear Father in heaven, when I get discouraged down here and heaven seems far away and the trials of earth are very real, please remind me of the day ahead when everything will be worth it. In Jesus' name. Amen.

HOPE FOR A ROBE

"It was granted her to clothe herself with fine linen, bright and pure"—for the fine linen is the righteous deeds of the saints.

REVELATION 19:8 ESV

Most of us are quite curious about heaven and eternity and all the details about our life there. There is only a little bit of information given. But the Bible does indicate that we will receive white robes. Whether we will wear these all the time or only on certain occasions is not clear. But the robes are made of good quality linen, and they are bright and pure.

Whatever the other details of our heavenly existence will be, we just may have to wonder until we get there. But one thing we know—He has everything well in hand.

* *

*Father, thank You for taking care of all the details
of my eternal home, even what I will wear. Amen.*

HOPE FOR A CITY

*And I saw the holy city, new Jerusalem, coming
down out of heaven from God, prepared
as a bride adorned for her husband.*

REVELATION 21:2 ESV

There are country-dwelling folks down here who wouldn't live
in a city for any amount of money. There are city-dwelling folks
down here who wouldn't take an airplane to travel somewhere.
But, in heaven, both will be satisfied and supremely happy.

The Bible does record that the New Jerusalem is a city. But
it will be a good city with no crime and no dirt, friendly people
and absolutely firm rules on citizenship. You will love it. Let's
stay faithful to Christ as we wait for Him to appear.

. . . .

*O God, You are the Architect of the universe and my
body and all of nature. The city You're preparing must be
wonderful! Thank You for making heaven beautiful. Amen.*

HOPE FOR A WEDDING

"Let us rejoice and exult and give him the
glory, for the marriage of the Lamb has come,
and his Bride has made herself ready."

REVELATION 19:7 ESV

Many women have not had the opportunity to experience a wedding on earth, but if they love and obey Jesus, the biggest wedding of all awaits them. The New Testament uses beautiful wedding imagery in the description of the betrothal (the Last Supper) and in the relationship Jesus described in His parables. In Ephesians, the apostle Paul, divinely inspired, described the glorious mystery comparing earthly marriage to Christ and the Church. There will be a great wedding feast, and the Bridegroom will be united forever with His bride. And the celebration will never end.

• •

Thank You, O Father, for giving Jesus to love and redeem me.
I look forward to the eternal wedding in the skies. Amen.